The Economic Basis
of Politics

CHARLES A. BEARD

The Economic Basis of Politics

New York

ALFRED · A · KNOPF

1947

THIS IS A BORZOI BOOK,
PUBLISHED BY ALFRED A. KNOPF, INC.

Manufactured in the United States of America

Published April 1922. Reprinted twice. Second edition, with a new preface by the author, published February 1934. Third edition revised, with a new preface and an additional chapter, published August 1945; reprinted twice. Fourth printing, June 1947.

The main body of this book consists of four lectures which I gave at Amherst College in 1916 on the Clark Foundation. These lectures—the fourth materially revised—were first published in 1922. Since that year the volume has been reprinted several times and a demand for it continues.

But during the past twenty-five years profound changes have occurred in the realities and ideas of Economics and Politics. So I have added a long chapter in which I deal with the bearings of recent historical events on the economic basis of politics, reconsidered the theory in the light of present circumstances, and restated it in formulas more in accord with contemporary experiences. I have, however, kept the text of the lectures as originally published in 1922. If I were re-writing them now I should make several modifications in details and in modes of expression; but, it seems to me, a writer does not treat his readers fairly if he leads them to imagine that he thought in 1916 or 1922 exactly as he thinks in 1945. Accordingly, I have only added a few foot-notes to the text of 1922; and I have enclosed them in brackets to indicate that they are new. Thus no confusion need arise in respect of the alterations and additions that have been made for this edition.

CHARLES A. BEARD

New Milford, Conn.,
Spring, 1945.

Contents

I. THE DOCTRINES OF THE PHILOSO-
PHERS   1

II. ECONOMIC GROUPS AND THE
STRUCTURE OF THE STATE   29

III. THE DOCTRINE OF POLITICAL
EQUALITY   46

IV. THE CONTRADICTION AND THE
OUTCOME   62

V. ECONOMICS AND POLITICS IN OUR
REVOLUTIONARY AGE   71

The Economic Basis
of Politics

The Doctrines of the Philosophers

THE FOUNDERS OF THIS LECTURESHIP DESIRE TO HELP carry forward the eternal quest of mankind for ways and means with which to control its social destiny for noble ends. Some of the most splendid traditions of the race are associated with this search. The mystic Plato, the sagacious Aristotle, the gentle Sir Thomas More, and the courageous Condorcet, to mention none nearer our time, sought far and wide for the key to the great mystery. The fruits of their labors are a priceless heritage.

The imperious Burke likewise thought the theme worthy of his talents, but he soon gave it up, confessing defeat. "I doubt," he says, "whether the history of mankind is yet complete enough, if it ever can be so, to furnish ground for a sure theory on the internal causes which necessarily affect the fortune of a state. I am far from denying the operation of such causes: but they are infinitely uncertain, and much more obscure and much more difficult to trace than the foreign causes that tend to raise, to depress, and sometimes to overwhelm a community. It is often impossible, in these political inquiries, to find any proportion between the apparent force of any moral causes we may assign and their known operation. We are therefore obliged to deliver up that operation to mere chance, or, more piously (perhaps, more rationally), to the occasional interposition and irresistible hand of the Great Disposer." In short, confronted by the complex and bewildering facts of social life, Burke cries aloud, with the mediaeval priest overwhelmed by the horror of the Black Death, "Deus vult."

In the field of natural science, such a confession is a plea of intellectual bankruptcy. In that sphere persistent and penetrating research, relentless and unafraid, brings about the progressive conquest and subjugation of the material world. Indeed the very research in mechanics and chemistry that produced the machine age has torn asunder the foundations of the old social order, released new and terrifying forces, and now threatens the dissolution of society itself. The present plight of the world seems to show that mankind is in the grip of inexorable forces which may destroy civilization if not subdued to humane purposes. It may be that in the end we must, with Burke, confess the futility of our quest. Even then we shall say with Heine:

> Also fragen wir beständig
> Bis man uns mit einer Handvoll
> Erde endlich stopft die Mäuler,
> Aber ist das eine Antwort?

So the eternal search goes on. At the very outset the seekers are confronted by two conflicting theories concerning the problem itself. These are summed up by John Stuart Mill at the opening of his famous work on representative government. According to one of them, government, namely, human control, is merely a problem in invention, of determining what is best and adapting our means to the desired end. According to the other theory, government is not a matter of human choice at all but an inevitable, natural growth in which the purposes of man have no part.

Each of these doctrines, we must admit with Mill, is untenable if pushed to an exclusive and logical conclusion; yet somewhere between them lies important truth. Long the victim of material forces, man has, by taking thought, made himself master of wind and wave and storm. May he not, by taking thought, lift himself above the social conflicts that destroy civilizations and make himself master of his social destiny? Perhaps not; but as the human mind is greater than the waterfall which it compels or the lightning's flash which it confines, so the control of human destiny is a nobler object of inquiry than the search for material power. Even though every door be slammed in our faces, still must we knock.

As the theme is old, we, as humble students, must, of necessity, first survey the conclusions of the great masters who have gone on before. We must first find out what they thought about the nature of the forces which are responsible for the origins, forms, and changes of political institutions.

At the beginning of such an inquiry we face, of course, the mighty Aristotle, "the master of all them that know." He rightly deserves to be called "the father of political science" because he took it out of the sphere of utopian idealism where Plato left it and placed it on the strong foundation of natural history. As Oncken rightly says, it was the use of the methods of natural science in his inductive studies that enabled Aristotle to make his great contribution to Greek thought. He was the son of a doctor who had written many books on medicine and physiology and he was himself no mean student of morphology and anatomy. Moreover he combined practical experience in politics with long and wide-reaching researches in the history of human institutions. It is for these reasons, perhaps, that Aristotle stood midway between those who thought that human society was a mechanism to be refashioned at will and those who accepted good and ill as fatalities of the gods. At all events we know that he sought to combine the idealism of ethics with the realism of historical research.

The most striking thing about Aristotle's *Politics* is the sharp contrast which it presents to most modern books on the same subject. The latter deal mainly with the structure and forms of government, the machinery and methods of elections, the powers and duties of public officers. The texture of society itself is left to the sociologist. The production and distribution of wealth, the foundations of human life, are assigned to the economist.

The reasons for this somewhat arbitrary carving up of the social organism for the purposes of study are not difficult to discover. Adam Smith and the older writers spoke of "Political Economy." About the middle of the nineteenth century, thinkers in that field were mainly concerned with formulating a mill owner's philosophy of society; and mill owners resented every form of state interference with their "natural rights." So "political economy" became "economics." [1] The state was regarded as a badge of original sin, not to be mentioned in economic circles. Of course, it was absurd for men to write of the production and distribution of wealth apart from the state which defines, upholds, taxes, and regulates property, the very basis of economic operations; but absurdity does not restrain the hand of the apologist.

To this simple historical explanation must be added another. This is an age of intense specialization. Every field of human knowledge is so vast that the workers therein are driven, in their endeavor to see things as they really are, further and further into the details of their subject. They then easily forget the profound truth enunciated by Buckle that the science of any subject is not at its centre but at its periphery where it impinges upon all other sciences. So the living organism of human society as a subject of inquiry has been torn apart and parcelled out among specialists.

Aristotle, in contrast, combines economics, politics and ethics. He considers the nature and function of the family before he takes up the forms of state. He then moves to the subject of property in its human relationships and considers the limits of communism and individualism. He rejects the former as impossible but he tells us that "poverty is the parent of revolution and crime." At no time does he lose sight of ethics. The aim

---

[1] [The history of the transition from "political economy" to "economics" has not yet been written. It is, of course, far more complex than my summary statements indicate.]

of the family and of property, as of the state, is the best life. Property as a means of getting more property or as an end in itself is inconceivable to him as a philosopher. Its aim is to enable man to live temperately and well, and this aim should determine the amount which each citizen ought to hold.

Having surveyed the family and property and the production and distribution of wealth—the texture of society—Aristotle proceeds to the consideration of the forms and nature of government, the causes of revolutions, and the conditions which favor the best society of which human nature is capable. How sound is this, how wise, how much more scientific than our modern practice of dissection and distribution among specialists! So the first conclusion to be drawn from Aristotle is that he never for an instant dreamed that ethics, politics, and economics could be torn apart and treated as separate subjects. He would have said of such pseudo-sciences with Ruskin: "I simply am uninterested in them as I should be in a science of gymnastics which assumed that men had no skeletons. It might be shown on that supposition that it would be advantageous to roll students up into pellets, flatten them into cakes, or stretch them into cables; and that when these results were effected the re-insertion of the skeleton would be attended with various inconveniences to their constitutions." Aristotle simply could not imagine a treatise on the state that did not consider the whole man rather than a highly hypothetical man—man as a mere political animal. This is apparent in his treatment of every phase of his subject.

When he approaches the heart of the matter, namely, the causes of variations in the forms of the state, he immediately relates economics and politics. He declares that there must "necessarily be as many different forms of government as there are ranks in the society, arising from the superiority of some over others and their different situations. And these seem to be two, as they say of the winds: namely, the north and the south; and all the others are declinations from these. And thus in politics, there is the government of the many and the government of the few; or a democracy and an oligarchy. . . . A democracy is a state where the freemen and the poor, being the majority, are invested with the power of the state. An oligarchy is a state where the rich and those of noble families, being few, possess it." In commenting on this laconic explanation of the differences in the form of the state by reference to differences in wealth, Aristotle's distinguished editor, Jowett, remarks in an equally laconic fashion: "As the poor or the middle class, or the notables predominate, they divide the government among themselves."

As economic classes depend upon the character and distribution of property, and as the forms of state turn upon the predominance of classes, it would follow logically that alterations in the form of state must have some connection with the changing fortunes of classes. This is exactly the conclusion Aristotle reached after he had considered the forces and conditions which produce revolutions in the affairs of nations. "Political revolutions," he says, "spring from a disproportionate increase in any part of the state. . . . When the rich grow numerous or properties increase, the form of government changes into an oligarchy or a government of families. . . . Revolutions break out when opposite parties, e.g. the rich and poor, are equally balanced and there is little or nothing between them. . . . Revolutions in democracies are generally caused by the intemperance of demagogues who either in their private capacity lay information against rich men until they compel them to combine (for a common danger unites even the bitterest enemies) or, coming forward in public, stir up the people against them. The truth of this remark is proved by a variety of examples. At Cos the democracy was overthrown because wicked demagogues arose and the notables combined. . . . The democracy at Heraclea was overthrown shortly after the foundation of the colony by the injustice of the demagogues which drove out the notables, who came back in a body and put an end to the democracy." There are collateral and incidental causes of revolutions, but "the universal and chief cause" of revolutionary feeling is "the desire of equality, when men think they are equal to others who have more than themselves; or again, the desire of inequality and superiority when, conceiving themselves to be superior, they think they have not more but the same or less than their inferiors; pretensions which may or may not be just."

It can hardly be doubted that Aristotle, in spite of some confusion of thought, looks upon the character and distribution of wealth in society as the chief determining factors in fixing the form of state. It is equally clear that he finds the causes of revolutions in states in contests among those who have much, those who have little, and those who have no, property. This disparity in fortune is the fundamental condition of which the demagogue avails himself in order to stir up strife and overturn established orders. Another commentator, Mr. A. D. Lindsay, observes: "When we come to Aristotle's analysis of existing constitutions we find that while he regards them as imperfect approximations to the ideal, he also thinks of them as the result of struggles between classes. . . . And each class is thought of, not as trying to express an ideal, but as struggling to acquire power to maintain its position. . . . His analysis of the facts forces him to look upon them [the Greek states] as the scene of struggling factions. The causes of revolutions are not described as primarily changes in the conception of the common good, but changes in the military or economic power of the several classes in the state."

Having come, by an inductive study, to the conclusion that there is a fundamental relation between the form and fortunes of the state and the character and distribution of property among the population, Aristotle applies the doctrine in his inquiry into "what is the best constitution for most states and the best life for most men, neither assuming a standard of virtue which is above ordinary persons, nor an education which is exceptionally favored by nature and circumstances, nor yet an ideal state which is an aspiration only."

His opinion touching this point is clear and simple: "Now in all states there are three elements; one class is very rich, another very poor, and a third is a mean. It is admitted that moderation and the mean are best, and therefore it will clearly be best to possess the gifts of fortune in moderation; for in that condition of life men are most ready to listen to reason. . . . Those who have too much of the goods of fortune, strength, wealth, friends, and the like are neither willing nor able to submit to authority. . . . On the other hand, the very poor, who are in the opposite extreme, are too degraded. So that the one class cannot obey and can only rule despotically; the other knows not how to command and must be ruled like slaves. Thus arises a city not of freemen but of masters and slaves, the one despising, the other envying. . . . A city ought to be composed, as far as possible, of equals and similars; and these are generally the middle classes. Wherefore a city which is composed of middle class citizens is necessarily best governed; they are, as we say, the natural elements of a state. And this is the class of citizens which is most secure in a state, for they do not, like the poor, covet their neighbour's goods; nor do others covet theirs, as the poor covet the goods of the rich; and as they neither plot against others, nor are themselves plotted against, they pass through life safely."

When Aristotle takes up the problem of finding the best material for a democracy he is no less insistent upon the economic element as the fundamental factor. The safest and most enduring form of democracy is, in his opinion, that based upon agriculture. In such a state the people are compelled to work hard for a livelihood, they have little time for political intrigue and combinations, they do not covet the property of others, and they will endure in patience oligarchies or tyrannies if they are allowed to work and are not deprived of their lands or cattle. Next to an agricultural democracy, that of a pastoral people is best, for those who live by their flocks are in many ways similar to husbandmen and they are well fitted for war. The worst and most dangerous democracy of all is that founded on commerce, for there is no moral excellence in the employments of traders, mechanics and laborers. By virtue of their economic occupations, they are turbulent, instable, and easily the prey of demagogues.[2]

As Aristotle, first among the ancients, commands the attention of every student of politics, so Machiavelli, first among the moderns, arrests our interest. Like his Greek predecessor, he was a man of affairs and a painstaking searcher into the history of political institutions. During most of his active life he was in the public

[2] "The best material of democracy is an agricultural population; there is no difficulty in forming a democracy where the mass of the people live by agriculture or tending of cattle. Being poor, they have no leisure and therefore do not often attend the assembly, and not having the necessaries of life they are always at work, and do not covet the property of others. . . . Next best to an agricultural and in many respects similar are a pastoral people, who live by their flocks; they are the best trained of any for war, robust in body, and able to camp out. The people of whom other democracies consist are far inferior to them, for their life is inferior; there is no room for moral excellence in any of their employments, whether they be mechanics, traders, or labourers. . . . The last form of democracy, that in which all share alike, is one which cannot be borne by all states, and will not last long unless well regulated by laws and customs. The most general causes which tend to destroy this or other kinds of government have now been pretty fully considered." Here Aristotle evidently refers to Bk. V. ch. 5 where he ascribes revolutions in democracies to hatred stirred by demagogues against the rich.

service of Florence. He was familiar with the inner politics of the turbulent Italian states. To experience in domestic politics he added a knowledge of foreign affairs gathered from many difficult diplomatic negotiations and missions. As his voluminous writings attest, he was a profound student of history, politics, and diplomacy.

When he writes of states founded upon the sword, his task is simple. He has merely to reckon with military forces and devices. When he deals with the origins of civil principalities he follows in the path cut by Aristotle. "A principality," he says, "results either from the will of the people or that of the nobles according as one or the other prevails. For the nobles, seeing that they cannot resist the people, begin to have recourse to the influence and reputation of one of their own class, and make him a prince, so that under the shadow of his power they may give free scope to their desires. The people also seeing that they cannot resist the nobles, have recourse to the influence and reputation of one man and make him a prince so as to be protected by his authority."

In advising the prince, once established, how best to maintain his power, Machiavelli warns him to take account of the conflict of classes out of which political power springs and to balance one over against the other, leaning to the right or to the left as occasion demands. By this shifting of affections the prince can cause the passions and ambitions of each class to nullify those of the other and so keep himself secure in power. In times of peace even, the prince should give attention to the balance of classes. "As cities are generally divided into guilds and classes, he should keep account of these bodies and occasionally be present at their assemblies, and should set an example of his affability and magnificence; preserving, however always the majesty of his dignity."

If time permitted it would be interesting to survey the political philosophies of Bacon, Raleigh, Harrington,[3] Montesquieu, Burke, and a score of other great men who have speculated upon the origin, nature, and fortunes of the state; but there is a limit to our enterprise. Students familiar with their writings know how deep is the impress of economics upon them.

Still there is one more philosopher of the Old World who cannot be neglected. As we have, of necessity,

---

[3] More than a century after Machiavelli's death an English writer, James Harrington, in constructing his model commonwealth, *Oceana*, gave to idealists the same advice that Machiavelli gave to the prince, namely that they should take into account the fact that the forms and distribution of property in society determine the nature of the state. "Dominion," he wrote, "is property, real or personal; that is to say, in lands, or in money and goods. Lands or the parts and parcels of a territory are held by the proprietor or proprietors, lord or lords of it, in some proportion; and such (except it be in a city that has little or no land and whose revenue is in trade) as is the proportion or balance or dominion or property in land, such is the nature of the empire. If one man be sole landlord or own three parts in four, the state is an absolute monarchy. If a few or a nobility with a clergy be the landlords and overbalance the people to a like proportion, the state is an oligarchy or a mixed monarchy. If the whole people be landlords or the lands are so divided among them that no man or aristocracy of men overbalance the many then the state is a commonwealth or anarchy." In short, political power follows property and it is the function of the statesman to see that property is not too narrowly concentrated, that a substantial landed class be maintained as the basis or stabilizer of the state.

examined the opinions of Aristotle and Machiavelli, so must we, of equal necessity, look into the writings of John Locke. He was, in a serious way, the forerunner of the American and French revolutions as well as the supreme apologist for the English revolution of 1688. All the great French critics of the old régime from Voltaire to Condorcet were familiar with their Locke. His works were translated into French for the benefit of those not familiar with his native tongue. Everywhere in the English colonies in America, students of politics were also acquainted with the philosopher of the Glorious Revolution. From him Jefferson drew both inspiration and guidance. Parts of the Declaration of Independence are merely paraphrases of passages in Locke's *Two Treatises on Government*. Like Aristotle and Machiavelli, this English thinker combined literary pursuits with practical affairs, although it must be said that his first-hand experience with politics is not to be compared with that of the Greek or the Italian.

Both the origin and end of the state Locke finds in the roots of property. "To avoid these inconveniences which disorder men's property in the state of nature," he writes, "men unite into societies, that they may have the united strength of the whole society to secure and defend their properties and may have standing rules to bound it, by which every one may know what is his. . . . The reason why men enter into society is the preservation of their property, and the end why they choose and authorize a legislature is that there may be laws made and rules set as guards and fences to the properties of all the members of the society." As the origin of the state is to be found in the requirements of property owners, so is the end of the state to be sought in the same source. "The great and chief end, therefore, of men's uniting into commonwealths and putting themselves under government is the preservation of their property."

As the preservation of property is the origin and end of the state, so it gives the right of revolution against any government or authority that invades property. Such is the economic foundation of the ethics of revolt. "The supreme power cannot take from any man part of his property without his consent." If perchance this is done, the owners of property, the people, have the right to cast off the old form of government and to establish a new one that will observe the ends of civil society. This will not be undertaken, of course, for light and transient reasons, but when a long train of abuses menaces the privileges of property and person, the right of revolution may be exercised.

So far we have considered only Old World writers, and according to methods of thinking cherished in many quarters we might easily conclude that European philosophy has no application to us—a favoured people who live in a new dispensation of our own making. It cannot be denied that the social and economic conditions of Athens, feudal Europe, or the Stuart age were in many respects different from those prevailing in the United States. Still mankind here, as in the Old World, must struggle for existence and, allowing for the divergences in circumstances, we have no reason for assuming that the economic laws which governed in other times and other lands are without effect in this fortunate country. Certainly the founders of the American republic did not assume that in shaping our political institutions they could break with the experience and philosophy of the past. That will be discovered by any one who takes the trouble to read the records of the convention assembled at Philadelphia in 1787 to frame the Constitution of the United States.

Time does not permit even a casual survey of those voluminous documents. Nor is such a general inquiry necessary. By common consent it is recognized that James Madison was "the father of the Constitution." He was a profound student of history and government. He kept the most complete record of the debates in the federal convention that has come down to us. He spent his long life in public service and political activities. He was twice President of the American union, and was intimately acquainted with nearly all the great statesmen of his time. He was the adviser of Washington and the confidant of Jefferson. He knew at first hand the stuff of which governments are made. To a study such as we are now making his views are simply indispensable and he may speak for his contemporaries.

In a powerful essay written in defence of the Constitution of the United States—Number Ten of the Federalist,—Madison sums up his political science in such a clear and concise form that no one can mistake his meaning. The prime function of government, he says, is the protection of the different and unequal faculties of man for acquiring property. "From the protection of different and unequal faculties of acquiring property, the possession of different degrees and kinds of property immediately results." This inexorable economic fact is the basis of political fact. Madison goes on: "From the influence of these [different degrees and kinds of property] on the sentiments and views of the respective proprietors ensues a division of society into different interests and parties. The latent causes of faction are thus sown in the nature of man; and we see them everywhere brought into different degrees of activity, according to the different circumstances of civil society." Thus, in the opinion of the Father of the American Constitution, politics springs inevitably, relentlessly, out of economics. The *sentiments* and *views* which arise from the possession of different degrees and kinds of property form the stuff of so-called "political psychology."

After this statement of controlling principle, Madison moves to his next fundamental problem, namely, the effect of these differences in economic condition and in political psychology on the government and its operation. Here too he has no doubts. He admits that there are occasionally fanciful and frivolous causes of internal disturbances but he is quick to add that "the most common and durable source of factions [4] has been the various and unequal distribution of property. Those who hold and those who are without property have ever formed distinct interests in society. Those who are creditors and those who are debtors fall under a

[4] "Faction" was the common term in the eighteenth century for "political party."

like distinction. A landed interest, a manufacturing interest, a mercantile interest, with many lesser interests grow up of necessity in civilized nations and divide them into different classes actuated by different sentiments and views. The regulation of these various and interfering interests forms the principal task of modern legislation, and involves the spirit of party and faction in the necessary and ordinary operations of the government. . . . The causes of faction cannot be removed. . . . We well know that neither moral nor religious motives can be relied on as an adequate control."

Thus Madison holds that, owing to the nature of men, unequal distribution of property is unavoidable; that in every civilized society, there will be persons holding different kinds and amounts of property; that from their holdings will arise special sentiments and views; that from these differing sentiments will arise contending political parties; and that political parties will seek to accumulate a majority and control the state. This danger, majority rule, Madison said in the constitutional convention, was especially grave in view of the inevitable rise of a landless proletariat—a vast class of propertyless persons likely to be actuated by the same sentiments and therefore certain to assault the rights of the propertied classes. To secure the public good and private rights against the dangers of such a majority party bent on attacking the property of the minority, and at the same time preserve the spirit and form of popular government, he concluded, was the object toward which the framers of the Constitution of the

United States directed their skill and their energies.

In short, the fundamental purposes and ideals of a free government in the New World, by the iron necessity of circumstances could not be essentially different from those of the Old World or the Ancient World. If government here is different from government in other times and places it is mainly because the forms and distribution of property are different.

But it may be said that Madison was from a slave state where political power did in fact result from the possession of land and slaves and that he was reading into universal politics the conclusions drawn from local accidents. Such a conclusion would of course be unjust to the great Virginian because all through his works there are the evidences of erudition which mark him out as one of the most learned men of his day. For a moment we may let the objection stand and inquire what were the views of some leading statesman and philosopher in the free North. Surely none will object if I choose a man who long and honorably represented the commonwealth of Massachusetts in the Senate of the United States and who found imperishable fame in the annals of his country, Daniel Webster. In a speech of great cogency and learning, delivered in the constitutional convention of his state in 1820, he defended the distribution of representation in the Senate on the basis of property. The principle of representing property, he said, was well established by writers of the greatest authority. Then he went on to expound his views with a show of learning and philosophy not often displayed in the American constitutional discussions.

"Those who have treated of natural law have maintained," he said, "as a principle of that law, that, as far as the object of society is the protection of something in which the members possess unequal shares, it is just that the weight of each person in the common councils should bear a relation and proportion to his interest. Such is the sentiment of Grotius, and he refers, in support of it, to several institutions among the ancient states.

"Those authors who have written more particularly on the subject of political institutions have, many of them, maintained similar sentiments. Not, indeed, that every man's power should be in exact proportion to his property, but that, in a general sense, and in a general form, property, as such, should have its weight and influence in political arrangements. Montesquieu speaks with approbation of the early Roman regulation, made by Servius Tullius, by which the people were distributed into classes, according to their property, and the public burdens apportioned to each individual according to the degree of power which he possessed in the government. By this regulation, he observes, some bore with the greatness of their tax because of their proportionable participation in power and credit; others consoled themselves for the smallness of their power and credit by the smallness of their tax.

"One of the most ingenious of political writers is Mr. Harrington, an author not now read as much as he deserves. It is his leading object, in his *Oceana*, to prove, that power *naturally* and *necessarily* follows property. He maintains that a government founded on property

is legitimately founded; and that a government founded on the disregard of property is founded in injustice, and can only be maintained by military force. 'If one man,' says he, 'be sole landlord, like the Grand Seignior, his empire is absolute. If a few possess the land, this makes the Gothic or feudal constitution. If the *whole people* be landlords, then it is a commonwealth.' 'It is strange,' says an ingenious person in the last century, 'that Harrington should be the first man to find out so evident and demonstrable a truth as that of property being the true basis and *measure* of power.' In truth, he was not the first. The idea is as old as political science itself. It may be found in Aristotle, Lord Bacon, Sir Walter Raleigh, and other writers. Harrington seems, however, to be the first writer who has illustrated and expanded the principle, and given to it the effect and prominence which justly belong to it. To this sentiment, Sir, I entirely agree. It seems to me to be plain, that, in the absence of military force, political power naturally and necessarily goes into the hands which hold the property. In my judgment, therefore, a republican form of government rests, not more on political constitutions, than on those laws which regulate the descent and transmission of property. . . .

"If the nature of our institutions be to found government on property, and that it should look to those who hold property for its protection, it is entirely just that property should have its due weight and consideration in political arrangements. Life and personal liberty are no doubt to be protected by law; but property is also to be protected by law, and is the fund out of which

the means for protecting life and liberty are usually furnished. We have no experience that teaches us that any other rights are safe where property is not safe. Confiscation and plunder are generally, in revolutionary commotions, not far before banishment, imprisonment, and death. It would be monstrous to give even the name of government to any association in which the rights of property should not be completely secured. The disastrous revolutions which the world has witnessed, those political thunderstorms and earthquakes which have shaken the pillars of society to their very deepest foundations, have been revolutions against property.

"The English Revolution of 1688 was a revolution in favor of property, as well as of other rights. It was brought about by men of property for their security; and our own immortal Revolution was undertaken, not to shake or plunder property, but to protect it. The acts which the country complained of were such as violated the rights of property. An immense majority of all those who had an interest in the soil were in favor of the Revolution; and they carried it through, looking to its results for the security of their possessions."

In another address, equally cogent, delivered on the anniversary of the landing of the Pilgrims, Webster applied the economic interpretation of politics directly to American institutions. "Our New England ancestors," he said, "brought thither no great capitals from Europe; and if they had, there was nothing productive in which they could have been invested. They left behind them the whole feudal policy of the other continent. . . .

They came to a new country. There were as yet no lands yielding rent, and no tenants rendering service. The whole soil was unreclaimed from barbarism. They were themselves either from their original condition, or from the necessity of their common interest, nearly on a general level in respect to property. Their situation demanded a parcelling out and division of the lands, and it may be fairly said that this necessary act *fixed the future frame and form of their government*.[5] The character of their political institutions was determined by the fundamental laws respecting property. . . . The consequence of all these causes has been a great subdivision of the soil and a great equality of condition; the true basis, most certainly, of popular government."

Having thus laid the foundations of politics in economics, Webster went on to give a warning and a prophecy. "The freest government," he said, "if it could exist, would not be long acceptable, if the tendency of the laws were to create a rapid accumulation of property in few hands and to render the great mass of the population dependent and penniless. In such a case, the popular power must break in upon the rights of property, or else the influence of property must limit and control the exercise of popular power. Universal suffrage, for example, could not long exist in a community where there was great inequality of property. The holders of estates would be obliged in such case either in some way to restrain the right of suffrage, or else such right of suffrage would ere long divide the property."

[5] Italics are Webster's own.

It is to be regretted that time does not permit the reading of these remarkable speeches in full, but we may summarize all of Webster's conclusions in the following manner:

1. The form of a government is determined (except where the sword rules) by the nature and distribution of property.

2. Republican government rests upon a wide distribution of property, particularly in land.

3. Government to be stable must be founded on men's interest.

4. Property to be secure must have a direct interest, representation, and check in the government.

5. Disturbances in countries arise principally from the conflict of groups resulting from variations in the form and distribution of property.

6. Universal suffrage is incompatible with great inequality of wealth.

7. Political wisdom requires the establishment of government on property and the control of its distribution through the regulation of alienage and transmission.

Far away in South Carolina, one of Webster's distinguished contemporaries, John C. Calhoun, reached substantially the same conclusions as he pondered upon the rise and fall of states and the problems of statecraft. Like his antagonist in the forum, he had his mind fixed upon the instant need of things—the defence of the special interest for which he was the leading spokesman; but in his quest for power he also sought for the inherent nature of things. Quickly his penetrating glance shot through the texture of political rhetoric to the underlying economic facts.

"If the whole community had the same interests," he declared, "so that the interests of each and every portion would be so affected by the action of the government, that the laws which oppressed or impoverished one portion, would necessarily oppress and impoverish all others,—or the reverse,—then the right of suffrage, of itself, would be all-sufficient to counteract the tendency of the government to oppression and abuse of its powers; and, of course, would form, of itself, a perfect constitutional government. The interest of all being the same, by supposition, as far as the action of the government was concerned, all would have like interests as to what laws should be made, and how they should be executed. All strife and struggle would cease as to who should be elected to make and execute them. The only question would be, who was most fit; who the wisest and most capable of understanding the common interest of the whole. This decided, the election would pass off quietly, and without party discord; as no one portion could advance its own peculiar interest without regard to the rest, by electing a favourite candidate.

"But such is not the case. On the contrary, nothing is more difficult than to equalize the action of the government, in reference to the various and diversified interests of the community; and nothing more easy than to pervert its powers into instruments to aggrandize and enrich one or more interests by oppressing and impoverishing the others; and this too, under the operation of laws, couched in general terms;—and which, on their face, appear fair and equal. Nor is this the case in some particular communities only. It is so in all; the small and the great,—the poor and the rich,—irrespective of pursuits, productions, or degrees of civilization; —with, however, this difference, that the more extensive and populous the country, the more diversified the condition and pursuits of its population, and the richer, more luxurious, and dissimilar the people, the more difficult is it to equalize the actions of the government,— and the more easy for one portion of the community to pervert its powers to oppress, and plunder the other.

"Such being the case, it necessarily results, that the right of suffrage, by placing the control of the government in the community must, from the same constitution of our nature which makes government necessary to preserve society, lead to conflict among its different interests,—each striving to obtain possession of its powers, as the means of protecting itself against the others;—or of advancing its respective interests, regardless of the interests of others. For this purpose, a struggle will take place between the various interests to obtain a majority, in order to control the government. If no one interest be strong enough, of itself, to obtain it, a combination will be formed between those whose interests are most alike;—each conceding something to the others, until a sufficient number is obtained to make a majority. The process may be slow, and much time may be required before a compact, organized majority can be thus formed; but formed it will be in time, even without preconcert or design, by the sure workings of that principle or constitution of our nature in which government itself originates. When once formed, the community will be divided into great parties,—a major and a minor,—between which there will be incessant struggles on the one side to retain, and on the other to obtain the majority,—and, thereby, the control of the government and the advantages it confers.

"So deeply seated, indeed, is this tendency to conflict between the different interests or portions of the community, that it would result from the action of the government itself, even though it were possible to find a community, where the people were all of the same pursuits, placed in the same condition of life, and in every respect, so situated, as to be without inequality of condition or diversity of interests. The advantages of possessing the control of the powers of the government, and, thereby, of its honours and emoluments, are, of themselves, exclusive of all other consideration, ample to divide even such a community into two great hostile parties."

It is evident from this review that the six great thinkers we have brought under consideration were in substantial agreement on the subject in hand. They believed that the fundamental factors with which the statesman has to deal are the forms and distribution of property and the sentiments and views arising from the possession of different degrees and kinds of property. Upon this generalization, we rest one of two conclusions. We may, upon reflection, decide that the distribution of property is the result of changeless forces inherent in the nature of man, and that the statesman is not a maker but an observer of destiny. Or we may hold that once the forces of social evolution are widely understood man may subdue them to his purposes. He may so control the distribution of wealth as to establish an ideal form of society and prevent the eternal struggle of classes that has shaken so many nations to their foundations. Man, the servant of fate, may become the master. But here we pause. Can the spirit of man be permanently enclosed in any system?

II

Economic Groups and the Structure of the State

HAVING SURVEYED THE THEORIES OF OUR SIX POLITICAL philosophers, it is fitting and proper that we should inquire whether there has been in fact a close relation between the structure of the state and the economic composition of society. It would be interesting, if time permitted, to examine the constitution of Athens and to consider such matters as Draco's legislation and Solon's reforms or to analyze the illuminating pages in which Polybius describes the balance of powers in Rome. The results of such a study, pondered in connection with the theories we have just reviewed, could not fail to set in train a fascinating line of speculation. There are, however, limits to this undertaking, and we must confine our scrutiny to the modern state in its historical growth.

In reviewing the history of government in Western Europe, from the disintegration of the Roman Empire to the opening years of the nineteenth century, we discover that wherever the simple sword-won despotism of the war leader, prince or king, is supplemented or superseded by some form of representation, it is not the people, considered as abstract equal personalities, who are represented, but it is propertied groups, estates. We are told by that profound student of mediaeval

29

law, Dr. Stubbs, that the ideal toward which Europe
was slowly working in the middle ages, was a constitution under which each class was admitted to a share of
power and control, and national action determined by
the balance of forces thus combined.

This was not, as he admits, a conscious design by
which statesmen shaped their policies. Many forces and
circumstances contributed to the making of the representative system of estates. Sometimes it was the
resistance of a particular economic group to royal despotism that won for it a recognized share in the government. An example of this is afforded by the contest
which ended in the grant of *Magna Carta*. The barons
wrote their interest into the public law of England,
and secured it by obtaining the right of actual participation as a class in the control of government. At other
times kings, especially during wars of conquest or defence, found themselves straitened for funds, and they
called upon certain classes or groups of men to fill their
treasury. Such, for instance, was the origin of the English House of Commons. To the continued financial
necessity of English kings, particularly during the long
war with France, was due the extraordinary development in the power of the English Parliament. Whatever the circumstances in each particular case, the striking fact is that we find all over mediaeval Europe what
Dr. Stubbs calls, "National assemblies composed of
properly arranged and organized classes."

If we examine the constitution of England in the
middle ages we find, in fact whatever the theory, four
estates: the clergy, the baronage, the landed gentry,

and the burgesses. Of these, the first three were founded, in the main, upon landed property. The first or spiritual estate in the English constitution comprised the whole body of the clergy. The clergy were invited to form a part of Parliament for two reasons. Their spiritual power was great, and even the boldest kings did not dare to defy them until the days of the mighty Henry VIII. But it is hardly to be doubted that it was as holders of property of immense value that the clergy came to a large share of the sovereign power. The bishops and the abbots, who were summoned to Parliament by name, were tenants-in-chief of the crown; in other words, they were great landed barons. As such they sat in the House of Lords. The inferior clergy in England, unlike their French brethren, though duly summoned to take their place in the great council of the realm, refused to obey the summons and remained for centuries in a convocation of their own, voting taxes on their property independent of the Parliaments of the realm. Though the clerical order was thus divided, the high authorities of the church sitting in the House of Lords and the inferior clergy dealing with the crown directly, it was mainly as a body of landed proprietors that the spiritual estate shared in the government.

The second English estate was the lay baronage, the members of which sat by their own right in the House of Lords along with the spiritual peers from the clerical estate. It is not necessary to inquire here into the historical circumstances which resulted in drawing a line between the richer barons and the untitled landed gentry, nor into those vainly disputed points of law which have been raised in the search for the origin and exact nature of the property rights which entitled a peer to a seat in the upper House. Whatever the cause may have been, the fact clearly stands forth, as Dr. Stubbs says, that in the middle ages the great land owners, tenants-in-chief, or titled lords, who appeared in person at the Parliament, were separated by a broad line from the freeholders who were represented by the knights of the shire.

According to a custom consecrated by time, it is the fashion to speak of the House of Commons as representing a sort of third estate, the commonalty of the realm. A little antiquarian inquiry, however, shows that the term "commons" does not derive its meaning, as is often erroneously supposed, from any connection with "the common people." On the contrary it comes from the vague word *communitas* which was used in the middle ages to describe a political organism such as a county or chartered town. The House of Commons, therefore, was in reality the house of the *communitates*, composed of representatives of the gentry of the counties and the burgesses of the towns considered as collective bodies within their respective geographical areas. Strictly speaking, we find in the lower house of Parliament the spokesmen of two estates: the smaller landowners and the burgesses. In the early stages of parliamentary evolution, the agents sent by the burgesses were even treated as a separate house or estate, although the way in which they voted on measures is obscure. Later they were combined with the gentry.

It was one of the peculiarities of the English system that the Parliament was not constituted of three or four distinct orders. In France, as we shall see, there were three separate estates—clergy, nobility, and third estate. In Sweden there were four orders—clergy, nobility, burghers, and peasants. In both of these countries each order formed a separate chamber and acted as a collective body. In England, on the other hand, there were only two chambers in the political system, unless we treat the separate convocation of the clergy as a part of the political organism. The House of Lords combined the great landed lay barons with the great landed clerical barons. The House of Commons included burgesses from the towns and representatives of the landed gentry below the baronial line. Still, it is quite apparent, in spite of these combinations that the English constitution of the middle ages was a group system, resting upon a foundation of economic classes.[1]

The principles underlying this mediaeval system of class representation have never been entirely abandoned in England in favor of the theory of abstract individual equality. They were well understood by Harrington, Locke, and Burke. Indeed the British constitution of mediaeval origin remained substantially unchanged until 1832, when the first of the great series of parliamentary Reform Bills was enacted. Although

[1] It must not be forgotten that the mediaeval clergy had a large vested interest in the profession. In addition to the huge landed estates given by pious benefactors for religious purposes, the clergy as a class had a large revenue from fees of various kinds. Much of the opposition of the middle classes to the Catholic Church was economic in origin.

nearly half a century had elapsed since the French Revolution let loose its flood of liberty and equality doctrines, English reformers, even in 1832, remained unmoved. They widened the suffrage, it is true, but what they did in effect was to enfranchise, by a set of ingenious qualifications, another "estate" which had grown up with the advance of industry and commerce, namely, a body of middle class manufacturers and shop keepers. In vain did the English Chartists talk of "one man one vote," and universal manhood suffrage.

When the next generation of English reformers "shot Niagara," in 1867, they merely enfranchised another "estate"—the working classes of the great industrial centres. And when again in 1884 a new addition was made to the British constitution, another "estate" was enfranchised, the agricultural labourers. At no point was the tax paying or property notion abandoned by the English in favor of the rule that a man should be allowed to vote simply because he is what Carlyle called "an unfeathered biped."

After the era of individualism set in it was more difficult to trace the line between economic groups than it had been in the middle ages, but whoever reads the debates over the great reform bills in England can see that statesmen, at each period, had in mind not abstract human equality, but what Dr. Stubbs characterized as a constitution in which each class of society should be admitted to a share of power and control. The significance of this story for the political future of England, in view of the changed position of women in industry, particularly since the outbreak of the Great

War, can readily be seen by one who has eyes to see.[2]

Everywhere in mediaeval Europe, as in England, we find constitutions resting upon estates, assemblies representing various orders, classes, and conditions of men, except the rightless serf at the bottom of society. In the Cortes of Aragon sat the clergy, the great barons (*ricos hombres*), the minor barons or knights, and the burgesses of the towns. The old parliament of Scotland was composed of prelates, barons and the smaller townsmen. In the representative assemblies which sprang up in some German principalities and in Russia, the same idea of class representation prevailed.

In the economic foundations of her Constitution, mediaeval France differed in no fundamental way from the neighboring countries. The history of the French estates, local and general, offers to the student of political science an abundance of group phenomena for analysis and interpretation. The records of more than three hundred years copiously illustrate the operation of the group process; an added and very significant interest is given to the study by the rôle of the Estates General on the eve of the great Revolution.

As early as 1212, Simon de Montfort called a parliament to which he summoned bishops, nobles, and distinguished bourgeois. A few years later, there was held at Beziers an assembly of the three orders (*des trois ordres*) to give advice relative to provincial administrative organization. In 1254, by royal ordinance,

[2] This sentence may stand as written in 1916. Not until 1917, during the great "War for Democracy," did England establish a practically universal suffrage.

the Seneschal Beaucaire was instructed to take counsel with the prelates, the barons, the knights, and the representatives of the towns (*hominibus bonarum villarum*).

The first Estates General, or National Parliament, was held in France in 1303. This was speedily followed by other parliaments. Speaking of the session of 1308, a chronicler said that the king wished to have the advice and consent of men "of every condition in the realm."

Like all early national assemblies, the French Estates General met only on the call of the king, and the methods of election depended naturally upon the terms of the royal orders. Complicated and varying practices were adopted at different times and places, but the following general principles were commonly observed. The members of the two privileged classes, the high clergy and the nobility, were summoned in person. The important convents and chapters were invited to send delegates. Occasionally the regular and secular clergy of a diocese united to elect their deputies. The nobility of the lower order usually chose their representatives, but sometimes members of this group appeared in person. In the towns the delegates were elected—often under a widely extended suffrage, including, on some occasions, women voters. These orders of society were known collectively as the clergy, the nobility, and the third estate.

It was not thought necessary, however, that each order should be represented only by members of the group. In mediaeval practice, on the contrary, clerks, nobles, curates and canons were sometimes chosen to represent townsmen. Often laymen were selected to speak for the clergy. Again, we see farmers (*roturiers*) and clergy standing as the spokesmen for men of noble order. Again it happened, perhaps to save expense, that the same deputies represented clergy, nobility, and third estate. Whatever the process of selection, however, each class acted separately and developed a certain consciousness of identical interest. When, in 1543, the king sought to unite the three groups in a common election, he found that instead of mitigating the group conflicts he only sharpened them. In a little while he restored the old practice of separate elections.

The French Estates General continued to meet from time to time until 1614, when the last grand session previous to the eve of the Revolution was held. At this memorable meeting there broke out a conflict between the nobility and the third estate which foreshadowed the struggle that was destined, more than one hundred and fifty years later, to destroy the whole system. The violence of this session, and perhaps the conflict then raging in England between the Parliament and James I, served as a warning that the monarch should beware of nourishing a dangerous hostility among the national estates.

Whatever may have been the cause—with that we are not now concerned—no session of the Estates General was again called until 1788. In that year the king, being in desperate financial straits, once more summoned the representatives of the different economic groups, that could give him relief, to consider the state of the realm. Immediately the antiquarians busied themselves with historical researches in order to restore the ancient and honorable institution of class government in its old form.

To the Estates General of 1789, each estate—clergy, nobility, and third estate—sent its members and representatives. Then arose, as every one knows, a fateful struggle for power. The clergy and nobility, bent on preserving their dominion, insisted that the vote on measures should be taken by the houses, as three distinct orders. Thus they hoped to prevent the upper classes from being overwhelmed by the numerical majority of the third estate, which had twice as many representatives in the assembly as the other two estates combined. Every school history tells us of the deadlock which ensued, of Mirabeau's eloquence, of the Tennis Court Oath, and of the National Assembly which, by firm action, was substituted for the old three-class system. Had the clergy and the nobility been willing earlier to surrender some of their privileges, and concede to the third estate a fair portion of political power, the history of the desperate years that followed the peaceful revolution of 1789 might have been far different. By resisting to the breaking point, the clergy and the nobility were conquered and almost destroyed by the third estate.

Less significant for the history of the world, but by no means less interesting in itself, is the parliamentary development of Sweden. From very early times the constitution of that kingdom recognized and provided for the representation of four distinct classes, clergy, nobility, burghers, and peasants. In the constitutional reorganization which followed the disturbances of the French Revolution and the Revolutionary Wars, this system was kept intact. Each class was not only distinctly represented, but each class had a house of its own through which the interests of the group were expressed in the government. The great landlords appeared in person. The spiritual house included the bishops and a number of other persons chosen by the clergy, the universities, and the academy of sciences, respectively. The representatives of the middle class were elected by the properly qualified burghers of the towns and the mine owners. The representatives of the peasants were chosen by the landowning farmers and certain other members of the soil-tilling population. Each of the four houses of parliament deliberated alone and acted in the name of and for the class which it represented. Ingenious provisions were devised for obviating deadlocks. This four-class parliament was retained until 1866 when two houses took the place of the old system.

The principle of class representation, which had been adopted in the development of mediaeval governments, was taken over entirely by Austria in her constitutional reconstruction shortly after the middle of the nineteenth century. The Austrian upper house consisted, of course, of the nobility, whose economic foundation was the land. In the formation of the lower house, in 1860–1, representation was distributed among the several provinces of the realm and it was provided that

the quota to which each province was entitled should
be selected by the local legislatures from definite economic groups.

It was stipulated that the total number of deputies
to be chosen should be distributed among four distinct
"estates," namely, (1) the great landlords (except in
Trieste and Vorarlberg where no such class existed,
and in Dalmatia where the highest taxpayers were put
into this group), (2) the burghers of the cities, markets,
and industrial places, (3) the peasants of the rural com-
munes, and (4) the chambers of commerce. In 1873
indirect election was abandoned for direct election by
popular vote, but the system of class representation
remained intact. Twenty-three years later, that is, in
1896, the non-taxpayers and industrial proletariat were
admitted to a share in the government. It was provided
that seventy-two deputies, now added to the parliament, should be chosen by the voters in general, including those already members of other classes. This
system of group representation remained in force until
1907 when manhood suffrage was adopted.

In formulating a constitution after the Revolution
of 1848, the King of Prussia deliberately founded his
government upon a class system, as you all know from
your study of comparative politics. The voters of Prussia are divided into three classes: those who pay one-
third of the income taxes elect indirectly one-third of
the delegates to the Prussian Diet; those who pay a second third of the income taxes likewise elect a third of
the delegates; and finally, all the rest of the voters, who
constitute almost the entire electorate, choose the re-

maining third of the deputies. Thus the Prussian Parliament is made up of a House of Lords, representing the landed interests, and a House of Commons or Diet, representing in two-thirds of its membership the wealth of the kingdom, and in one-third the propertyless. Years of agitation and a threatened revolt on the part of the masses have failed to shake the foundations of this strongly knit system of class government.[3]

All this, you may think, is interesting enough, but without bearing upon American conditions. It may be said that whatever were the practices of mediaeval France, England, Sweden, and Aragon, they have no meaning for the United States founded under another dispensation. There stands the Declaration of Independence with its immortal statement that all men are created free and equal and that governments derive their just powers from the consent of the governed. Here is what seems to be a repudiation of the whole notion of class or group interest in the process of government; but when we turn from theory to fact we find ourselves in the midst of mediaeval forms and institutions.

An examination of the first American state constitutions reveals no abandonment of the Old-World notion that government rests upon property. Take, for instance, the Massachusetts constitution of 1780 drawn by John Adams and adopted after long and serious deliberation. In this document we discover that no man

[3] So things stood in 1916 when these lectures were given. This system was overthrown in the German Revolution of 1918. [After the advent of Hitler in 1933 the equalitarian political regime substituted for the old Prussian class-government was extinguished by force.]

could vote for members of the legislature or for governor, unless he had a freehold estate of the annual value of three pounds, or some estate of the value of sixty pounds. Here is a distinct recognition of two classes of property interests in the government—real property and personalty. To add further security to the two orders or "estates" the constitution provided that no one could be elected governor who did not possess a freehold of the value of one thousand pounds, and furthermore, that the senators should be distributed among the respective districts of the state on the score of the amount of taxes paid in each of them. It was in defence of this last provision that Daniel Webster made his famous speech in the Massachusetts convention of 1820, defending the economic basis of government. If the Massachusetts constitution proved to be rather democratic in its operations, that was, as Webster pointed out, due to the wide distribution of property, not to any desire of the Massachusetts Fathers to sacrifice the security of property to a political shibboleth.

If we take a great middle state like New York, we find that the constitution drafted in 1777 distinctly recognized the existence of classes by establishing the predominance of the farmers. It provided that the senate should be composed of freeholders, and that none but freeholders possessing one hundred pounds worth of land could vote for the senators or for governor. A slighter property qualification was placed upon voters for the lower house—a qualification which admitted freemen of the incorporated towns, renters, and a few others, but kept out the lower levels of the proletariat. This class system remained in vogue until 1821. It was abolished then only against the violent protests of many intellectual leaders of the time, such as Chancellor Kent, who maintained that the rights of property could be protected only when property was frankly represented in the government, and that those "without a stake in the country" should have no voice in its politics.

The Fathers of the South did not differ from those of the North. In the agricultural state of Virginia, where there were few merchants and capitalists, the predominance which the landed classes possessed in fact was also established in right. Only freeholders could vote in that state under the constitution of 1776, and this restriction was kept in force for more than half a century. When a vigorous but vain attempt was made, in the constitutional convention of 1829, to abolish it, the freehold suffrage was defended on the ground that the landed group was the only secure foundation for government because all other classes were variable and transitory in character, while the possession of land furnished the strongest evidence of permanent, common interest with, and attachment to, the community.

Admitting the plain evidence of the first state constitutions, that the wise founders of this Republic recognized the place of property interests in political processes, it may be said that the Constitution of the United States, drawn in that period, nowhere takes into account the existence of economic divisions. This is true, if we read merely the language of the instrument and not the records of the convention which drafted it. In the document itself there are no provisions similar to those which appear in the first state constitutions, placing landed- and personal-property qualifications on the suffrage and office holding; but the omission was not made because the framers of that immortal instrument were indifferent to the rights of property or unaware of the influence wielded by economic groups upon the course of government. Neither was it because they disapproved of property qualifications, for such existed in nearly every state in the Union. In fact property qualifications for officers and for voters were proposed in the convention, but it was impossible to agree on their precise form. Inasmuch as many of the troubles under the Articles of the Confederation had arisen from attacks on capital by state legislatures elected by freeholders, and inasmuch as the convention was especially eager to safeguard the rights of personal property, a freehold qualification did not seem to offer an adequate remedy. On the other hand, to impose a large personal-property qualification on voters would have meant the defeat of the Constitution by the farmers who were, of necessity, called upon to ratify it. Under the circumstances the framers of the Constitution relied, not upon direct economic qualifications, but upon checks and balances to secure the rights of property—particularly personal property—against the assaults of the farmers and the proletariat.[4]

At this point we may summarize. Our six political philosophers regarded property, in its various forms

[4] This subject is covered at length in my *Economic Interpretation of the Constitution*, pp. 152–168.

and distribution, and the social groups which arise out of economic processes, as the fundamental materials for the science of government. We have seen also that the constitutions of government of great nations were, for centuries, deliberately fitted to the division of society into separate orders, groups, and estates, each of which pursued a separate calling and cherished its own sentiments about economic interests.

This great fact stands out clearly, that through the centuries—down until our own day—group interests were recognized as forming the very essence of politics both in theory and practice. Statesmen spoke of them, negotiated with them, placated them, legislated for them, and sought generally to secure the predominance of one or the other or the balance of several against one or another. At all events, statesmen spoke not of abstract men and abstract rights, but of real men and real rights. What has happened to sweep away the practices of centuries, to challenge the philosophy of the world's greatest political thinkers, and to introduce the rule of "the people" instead of the rule of estates? Have the economic conditions of the world been revolutionized, the estates and orders abolished?

III

The Doctrine of Political Equality

THE GREAT POLITICAL PHILOSOPHERS, WITH FEW EXCEP-
tions, have regarded property as the fundamental element in political power, and have looked upon a
constitution as a balance of economic groups. The governments founded and developed before the nineteenth
century were in fact complexes of group interests. Nowhere was the representative system, in its origin, designed to reflect the opinions of mere numerical
aggregations of human beings considered in the abstract apart from property and employment. On the
contrary, it reflected the sentiments and views of different sorts and conditions of men, estates or orders:
clergy, nobility, burghers, and minor landowners.

In the United States where there was no clerical
estate or established nobility to be represented in the
government, the existence of the two fundamental
property groups—the owners of realty and the owners
of personalty—was taken into account either in posi-
tive constitutional law or in the check and balance system provided by the separation of powers.[1] If the first
American constitutions were more democratic than

[1] Much ingenuity has been spent by American lawyers in elaborating
the theoretical fictions of Montesquieu. The real significance of the
separation of powers and its relation to the balance of class interests

those of Europe, the fact is not to be attributed to radical changes in human nature, induced by a voyage across the Atlantic, but, as the great Webster pointed out, to a very wide distribution of property, due mainly to cheap land.

So things stood in the closing years of the old régime. Then suddenly came two great revolutions, one in economic fact, and the other in political theory. The first was brought about by the invention of the steam engine and machinery, creating an immense amount of property which had hitherto existed only as a minor element in economic life, namely, industrial and mercantile capital. So rapidly did this new form of property accumulate that even in the United States, by the middle of the nineteenth century, it exceeded in value the agricultural land of the country.

Being more mobile and more easily concentrated than land, a vast portion of it quickly fell into the hands of, relatively speaking, a small portion of society. As land was the great stabilizer of the old order, so capital became the great disturber in the new order. Like a mighty giant tossing to and fro in a fever, in its quest for profits, it tore masses of men from the land, from their sleepy villages and hamlets, and hurled them here and there all over the globe. Under its influence the old sharp class differences were disarranged. The peasant might become a successful cotton spinner, a financial magnate, a contributor to party war-chests, a peer

in society was appreciated by eighteenth century writers, but if more modern statesmen have understood them they have seldom been frank in setting forth their views.

of the realm. The Manchester individualists, Cobden and Bright, looking upon the new order which they had helped to create, pronounced it good and declared that because any hustling individual might rise from poverty to wealth, the era of *individual* equality had arrived. Instead of studying the new groups, the new class divisions, more subtle and complex than ever before, they proclaimed the glad day of equality. While James Watt was experimenting in Glasgow with the steam engine, and thus preparing to blow up the old economic order in the realm of fact, a French philosopher, Jean Jacques Rousseau, was experimenting with ideas scarcely less dangerous to the *ancien régime* than the operations of the Scotch mechanic. Unlike his distinguished predecessor in political science, Montesquieu, Rousseau did not search assiduously among the institutions and habits of mankind to find a basis for his political philosophy.[2] Rousseau was not a man of

[2] Montesquieu recognized the place of economic groups in his system of political economy:

"In a popular state the inhabitants are divided into certain classes. It is in the manner of making this division that great legislators have signalized themselves; and it is on this the duration and prosperity of democracy have ever depended. Servius Tullius followed the spirit of aristocracy in the distribution of his classes. We find in Livy and in Dionysius Halicarnassus, in what manner he lodged the right of suffrage in the hands of the principal citizens. He had divided the people of Rome into a hundred and ninety-three centuries, which formed six classes; and ranking the rich, who were in smaller numbers, in the first centuries; and those in middling circumstances, who were more numerous, in the next, he flung the indigent multitude into the last; and as each century had but one vote, it was property rather than numbers that decided the elections. Solon divided the people of Athens into four classes. In this he was directed by the spirit of democracy, his intention not being to fix those who were to choose, but such as were eligible: therefore, leaving to every citizen

science or a detached scholar. He was a passionate propagandist. He formulated the sentiments and views for the third estate in France then beginning to thunder against the monarchy, which was buttressed by the special privileges of the clergy and the nobility. In his *Social Contract* he set forth the moral and philosophic justification for the revolt of the third estate.

In his system of political thought, Rousseau, in effect, advanced several negative propositions. He denied that there was any inherent and essential connection between economics and politics. He repudiated the idea that the nature and amount of men's material possessions and the character of their occupations could have any substantial influence on their political sentiments and their political actions. He rejected the age-long view that the transmission, alienation, accumulation, and distribution of wealth bore a fundamental relation to the form and practices of the government. He denied the doctrine that society is a complex of more or less conscious groups and interests. For the group- or class-man he substituted the abstract, the cosmopolitan, the universal man.

In order that we may get the essence of this new political philosophy, let us make a somewhat close examination of the doctrines laid down by Rousseau. He simply cannot be ignored, for his *Social Contract* became the textbook of the French Revolution and of

the right of election, he made the judges eligible from each of those four classes; but the magistrates he ordered to be chosen only out of the first three, consisting of persons of easy fortunes."—Montesquieu, *The Spirit of Laws*, Vol. I, p. 10.

that world-wide equalizing movement which has in our day penetrated even the heart of China, preparing the way for the overthrow of absolutism and the triumph of the third estate.

The origin of the state Rousseau finds not in a divine command that one should rule over others, or in the fusion of estates, but in a voluntary union of free men. Of course Rousseau knows that this was not true in point of fact, and respect for the truth compels him to admit it. But he cannot allow the matter of historicity to interfere with the foundations of his system of political ethics.

In Book I of his *Social Contract*, he says: "If, then, we remove from the social contract all that is not of its essence, it will be reduced to the following terms: Each of us gives in common his person and all his force under the supreme direction of the general will; and in return we receive each member as an indivisible part of the whole.

"Immediately, this act of association produces, instead of the individual person of each contracting party, a moral and collective body, composed of as many members as the assembly has votes, which receives from the same act its utility,—its common being, its life and its will. This public personage, thus formed by the union of all the others, formerly took the name of city, and now takes that of republic or body politic. This is called the *state* by its members when it is passive; the *sovereign* when it is active; and a *power* when comparing it to its equals. With regard to the associates, they take collectively the name *people*, and call themselves individually *citizens*, as participating in the sovereign authority, and *subjects*, as submitted to the laws of the state. But these terms are often confounded and are taken one for the other. It is enough to know how to distinguish them when they are employed with all precision."

Having found the origin of society in a general agreement of free and equal men, Rousseau naturally places sovereign power by moral right in "the people"—a collectivity of all the individual members of the state. The law of the state is therefore not the will of some class (like the landed gentry) imposed upon all others, or a compromise rule produced by a balance of conflicting group interests, but is, according to Rousseau, an expression of "the general will." This alone is its justification.

Even if it destroys the rights and property of the individual still he must abide by it. "In order then that the social contract may not be an idle formula, it includes tacitly this engagement, which alone can give force to the others, that whoever shall refuse to obey the general will, shall be compelled to it by the whole body. This signifies nothing if not that he will be forced to be free; for it is this condition which, giving each citizen to the country, guarantees him from all personal dependence—a condition which forms the device and working of the political machine, and alone renders legitimate civil engagements which without that would be absurd, tyrannical, and subject to great abuse."

In the formulation of this general will, all individuals

share alike. Here Rousseau proclaims the doctrine of absolute political equality with a vengeance. If the state, he says, is composed of ten thousand citizens, then each member of the state has one ten-thousandth part of the sovereign authority. If the people is composed of one hundred thousand men, then the citizen's suffrage is reduced to a hundred-thousandth part, and he has obviously ten times less influence in the formation of the laws. Hence it follows, declares the philosopher, "that the larger the state becomes, the less liberty there is."

But Rousseau is face to face with the fact that unanimity among citizens is impossible and that the general will cannot be the will of the whole ten thousand or the whole hundred thousand, as the case may be, but must, perforce, be the will of a certain fraction of the citizens. He boldly meets the problem, and following the old philosophers he holds that the exercise of sovereignty is by the majority. The *general will* of which he makes so much, is in practice, the will of a majority. With fine confidence he contends that the will of the majority is right and works for the good of the state. The minority is wrong; it is nothing, because it follows from the nature of the social contract that the minority must accept the decrees of the majority. With the courage of his convictions, he says: "When, however, the opinion contrary to mine prevails, it only shows that I was mistaken, and that what I had supposed to be the general will was not general. If my individual opinion had prevailed, I should have done something other than I had intended, and then I should not have been free."

As he contemplates the consequences of this bold doctrine Rousseau shrinks a bit. There is a limit even to the self-abnegation of the reformer. In Chapter VI of the Fourth Book Rousseau safeguards the oppressed minority in certain fundamental matters by requiring an extraordinary majority of two-thirds—even three-fourths in some cases. But this is rather an afterthought, though a very serious one. It does not vitally affect his extreme doctrines of individualization. Neither did it check materially the fateful consequences of his general doctrine of universal male equality. Rousseau is aware of the dangers of mere numerical majorities, but he cannot escape altogether the results of his general levelling down. There is simply a limit to which he can allow the logic of his argument to carry him. Just as he excludes women from his "people" so he sets some metes and bounds to the doings of the mere majority.[3]

Nothing further need be said to show how revolutionary was Rousseau's doctrine for the old order, or for any order. Under it the rights and property of all groups and all classes become subject to the will of the numerical majority. Any system of government founded on a compromise, or a balance of interest, in defiance of mere numbers on the one side or the other, thus becomes not only indefensible, but immoral and undemocratic. Written to exalt the individual, it subjects him to a new tyranny—the will of a temporary

[3] Aulard contends that Rousseau was a *bourgeois* and in reality wished to exclude the propertyless as well as the women from his "people." Whether this is true or not, Rousseau's disciples, in the earlier stages of the Revolution, were not ready to throw away all property qualifications on the suffrage.

majority. For his sufferings in conscience or in property, it offers him the consoling information that his individual will, being contrary to the general will, is wrong, and, in fact, not his intention at all or in keeping with his own freedom!

Indeed, as we look at this system, it seems so unreal, so ill-adapted to the world of industry and trade, commerce and agriculture, that its implications are astounding. We can hardly imagine how it could become the philosophy of any people. An examination into the course of events, however, makes the explanation clear.

Naturally enough Rousseau's philosophy did not appeal to the French clergy and nobility, who were aware of their class interests and of their numerical inferiority. To them the social contract was poisonous and impious anarchy.

To the bourgeois, on the other hand, it presented a different aspect. They had grown powerful in numbers and wealth, and they felt keenly the oppressive privileges enjoyed by the clergy and nobility. They were determined to sweep away the discriminations against them, and to control the government in their own interests. If they did not contemplate the destruction of the clergy and the nobility as classes, they did contemplate levelling them down in their political and economic privileges. The clergy and the nobility had a monopoly of the philosophy of divine right—the moral support of their power. The bourgeois had to look elsewhere for a philosophy to justify such levelling as they contemplated. They found it in Rousseau's

Social Contract. Searching for an ethical support for their attack upon two powerful groups, they exalted "the people" as against all special privileges. They were playing with fire and they knew it, but there seemed no other philosophy at hand to serve as a foil for their enterprise. Unwittingly they started a conflict, the consequences of which will last until the end of time.

In the shock of the French Revolution the bourgeois overthrew the nobility and the clergy. They abolished the feudal rights of the former and seized the property of the latter. In their fear of the privileged orders they established a legislature of one chamber and sought to safeguard their property by a tax-paying qualification on the right to vote; but the logic of their position was fatal. They had proclaimed the rights of man as the moral justification for the destruction of the rights of two classes, and they had at the same time coolly repudiated the rights of man by limiting the application of the doctrine to members of their own class who had certain property qualifications.

Then followed the Revolution of violence and terror in which radical leaders inflamed the disfranchised by appeals to the gospel of Rousseau and to the proclamations of the bourgeois. To save themselves the latter had to resort to that other great source of authority, the sword. This instrument was wielded by Napoleon Bonaparte, a man who understood the relation of property to political power, and who, through his constitutions based on checks and balances, gave stability to bourgeois institutions. Even Napoleon, the Bourbons, and the Orleanists, however, could not stay the onward march of Rousseau and his legions.[4]

But it may be asked, how did this levelling doctrine of universal political equality find a foothold in the United States where there were no official clergy and nobility to be overthrown by the third estate? Well, some writers have laboured hard to show that it is a French creation utterly at variance with Anglo-Saxon tradition—whatever that may mean. In the interest of truth, however, it should be said that the free-and-equal doctrine is not French, but English in origin. Its beginnings among English-speaking peoples may be traced to the flood of speculation that broke loose in England during the seventeenth century when the merchants and gentry were engaged in a revolt against the crown and aristocracy—the clergy having been broken a century earlier by the bluff king, Henry VIII, who confiscated much of their property. It was from English defenders of revolution, like John Locke, rather than from French authors, that Jefferson derived the gospel of the Declaration of Independence. Moreover the economic circumstances in the United States were on the whole favorable to the propaganda of that word.

[4] In the Declaration of the Rights of Man—August 1789—the French National Assembly proclaimed in theory the political philosophy of Rousseau: "men are born and remain equal in rights," and "law is the expression of the general will." In the National Assembly it appears that only five deputies, however, asked for universal manhood suffrage—among them Robespierre, who was destined to ride the storm of the proletarian revolution which he fain would have tempered with a pale and sickly piety. It is estimated that under the first French Constitution about three-fifths of the adult males were deprived of the suffrage by the property qualifications established. Thus did the bourgeois mutilate the doctrines of Jean Jacques.

There was no established clergy here. There was no titled aristocracy. There was no such proletariat as formed the "mob" of Paris. Land was the chief form of property and its wide distribution among the whites (leaving the slaves out of account) brought about in fact a considerable economic equality to correspond to the theory of political equality.

Moreover, at the time that America was committed to the theory of political equality, the people were engaged in a revolt against the government imposed on them under the authority of Great Britain. Like the third estate in France they needed some effective and compelling justification for their extraordinary conduct. Of course the leaders of the American Revolution could have said coldly: "We are fighting for the plantation owners of the South, the merchants and landed gentry of the North, and the free farmers in both sections, in order that they may govern themselves."

Obviously, such a chilly declaration of fact would not have thrilled the masses, especially the mechanics of the towns who enjoyed no political rights under either system, the old or the new. It was necessary to have something that would ring throughout the country. Hence the grand words of the Declaration of Independence: "All men are created equal" and "governments derive their just powers from the consent of the governed." There were critics ready to point out that these high principles did not square with slavery, indentured servitude, and political disfranchisement, but they did not prevail. In the fervor of the moment, Jefferson, while bent on justifying the revolt against George III, in fact challenged the rule of property which was guaranteed by the state constitutions drafted by his fellow revolutionists in that very epoch. Even Jeffersonians, when confronted, like Rousseau's followers, with the logical consequences of their doctrine shrank from applying it. Nevertheless the grand words stood for all time, and advocates of manhood suffrage and woman suffrage afterward appealed to them with great effect in attacking property and sex qualifications on the right to vote.

When once the free-and-equal doctrine had been let loose in the New World and the Old, it was impossible to check its course. Steadily it made headway against governments founded upon a class basis. Steadily it supplanted the old philosophy of politics which gave to property and to estates a place in the process of government. Within seventy years after the Declaration of Independence the battle for white manhood suffrage was virtually won in the United States. Some remnants of the old system of class privilege in politics remained, but they were regarded as anachronisms. Time was to dispose of them. America was committed to the great doctrine that in politics all heads are equal and all are entitled to the same share of power in the government.

In Europe also political equalitarianism has done deadly work in the old order. In England it has not been carried to the same degree as in the United States, but the Lords' Veto Act, levelling down the power of the ancient and honorable Chamber of Peers, is an echo of it, full of significance for the future.[5] In Sweden, in 1866, the four-class system was swept away in favor of a general suffrage. Austria abandoned group representation in 1907. The third French Republic abolished the Chamber of Peers and substituted a Senate, now chosen by indirect election. At this moment China is in the throes of a Revolution due to the struggle between those who would establish a stable government on the foundations of effective economic and military interests, and those fired with a passion for "the rights of man."

The logical application of Rousseau's doctrine of complete and abstract human equality is clear. It means that the number of members in any legislature shall be apportioned among geographical districts approximately according to the number of inhabitants without reference to their wealth, occupations, or interests. It means that all high public officers shall be elected by majorities or pluralities. Man is to be regarded as a "political" animal. No account is to be taken of those senti-

[5] The suffrage act of 1917, passed after this was written, carried England into Rousseau's camp. The revolution that followed the German defeat in 1918 swept Germany and the new continental states into the main current. Russia, however, went back to the class system while attempting to abolish the clergy, the nobility, and the bourgeois as classes. [Nearly all the democratic governments set up in Europe after the First World War were destroyed by dictators within a brief span of years. See below, p. 73. The Bolshevik class system of councils representing workers, peasants, and soldiers underwent many changes before a final constitution was adopted in 1936. Under that constitution, the All-Union Congress represents population and nationalities. Theoretically there are now no classes in Russia. See below, p. 85.]

ments and views which, as Madison says, arise from the possession of different degrees and kinds of property. All heads are equal and, from the point of view of politics, alike. The statesman is a mathematician concerned with counting heads. The rule of numbers is enthroned. The homage once paid to kings is to be paid to the statistics of election returns. Surely, in all the history of thought, there is nothing more wonderful than this "logic of democracy."

While this political revolution has been going on, have the economic groups once recognized by statesmen and political philosophers disappeared? The answer is emphatic. It is to be found in the census returns, which, as certainly as the doomsday book of William the Conqueror, record the perdurance of group and class interests despite the rhetoric of political equality. It is to be found in practical politics day by day. Does any one think that a thousand farmers or laborers, going on about their tasks, have the same influence in the formation of a protective tariff bill as a thousand manufacturers represented by spokesmen in the lobbies and committee rooms of the Congress of the United States? Does any one suppose that the exemption of trade unions from the provisions of the Sherman Anti-Trust Law was the result of the platonic wishes of "the people," rather than the determined and persistent activity of The American Federation of Labor?

We are therefore confronted by an inherent antagonism between our generally accepted political doctrines, and the actual facts of political life. In the world of natural science men do not tarry long with hypotheses that will not square with observed phenomena. Shall we in the field of political science cling to a delusion that we have to deal only with an abstract man divorced from all economic interests and group sentiments?

IV

The Contradiction and the Outcome

THREE GENERAL CONCLUSIONS WERE REACHED IN THE preceding chapters. A survey of six great systems of political philosophy supports the proposition that there is a vital relation between the forms of state and the distribution of property, revolutions in the state being usually the results of contests over property. A study of the evolution of government in western civilization during many centuries shows the recognition of economic classes in the creation of political organisms. Finally, modern equalitarian democracy, which reckons all heads as equal and alike, cuts sharply athwart the philosophy and practice of the past centuries.

Nevertheless, the democratic device of universal suffrage does not destroy economic classes or economic inequalities. It ignores them. Herein lies the paradox, the most astounding political contradiction that the world has ever witnessed. Hence the question arises: Has political democracy solved the problem of the ages, wrung the answer from the sphinx? Is it a guarantee against the storms of revolution? Does it make impossible such social conflicts as those which tore ancient societies asunder? Does it afford to mankind a mastery over its social destiny?

To ask these questions is to answer them.[1] Nothing was more obvious in the thinking of western civilization before the outbreak of the World War than dissatisfaction with political democracy. Equally obvious was the discontent with representative government based on the doctrine of abstract numbers and civic equality. Whether one went into the countryside of Oregon or strolled along Quai d'Orsay, one heard lively debates over "the failure of representative government." The initiative and referendum and recall—direct government—more head counting on the theory of numbers and abstract equality, such was the answer of the Far West to the riddle. Europe had another answer, or rather many other answers.

Indeed, John Stuart Mill, in his work on representative government published in 1859, nearly ten years before the radical suffrage measure of 1867, sensed grave dangers ahead. He utterly rejected the theory that political democracy would inevitably avoid those acts of selfishness and arbitrary power that had characterized monarchies and oligarchies and aristocracies. "Looking at democracy in the way in which it is commonly conceived," he said, "as the rule of the numerical majority, it is surely possible that the ruling power may be under the dominion of sectional or class interests pointing to conduct different from that which would be dictated by impartial regard for the interest of all. . . . In all countries there is a majority of poor, a minority who, in contradistinction, may be called rich. Between these

[1] This lecture has been re-written since the close of the World War, but the main conclusions have not been altered.

two classes, on many questions, there is a complete opposition of interest. We will suppose the majority sufficiently intelligent to be aware that it is not to their advantage to weaken the security of property, and that it would be weakened by any act of arbitrary spoliation. But is there not considerable danger lest they should throw upon the possessors of what is called realizable property and upon larger incomes, an unfair share, or even the whole of the burden of taxation; and having done so, add to the amount without scruple, expending the proceeds in modes supposed to conduce to the profit and advantage of the labouring class?" Mill then goes on to cite other examples of the possible abuse of political power in the interests of the ecomonic classes.

His solution of the problem was a balance of classes and the introduction of minority or proportional representation. "If the representative system could be made ideally perfect," he said, "and if it were possible to maintain it in that state, its organization should be such that these two classes, manual labourers and their affinities on one side, employers of labour and their affinities on the other, should be, in the arrangement of the representative system, equally balanced, each influencing about an equal number of votes in Parliament." The more rational minority in each class should then hold the balance. "Assuming that the majority of each class, in any differences between them, would be mainly governed by their class interests, there would be a minority of each in whom that consideration would be subordinate to reason, justice, and the good of the whole; and this minority of either joining with the whole of the other, would turn the scale against any demands of their own majority which were not such as ought to prevail."

Whether this solution is fanciful or sound need not detain us now. The point is that this learned and sincere friend of democracy, writing at the middle of the nineteenth century, believed that the introduction of "numerical democracy" had not solved and could not resolve the most fundamental of all contradictions: namely the contests over property and the distribution of wealth that accompany the development of civilization. Indeed Mill's very solution, minority representation, in effect was designed to re-introduce, without rigid legal divisions, the scheme of class representation which had been for centuries the basis of all parliamentary systems. On the significance of this it is not necessary to comment.

Long after Mill's day a group of continental writers, Leon Duguit, Charles Benoist, and Albert Schaeffle, for example, declared the system of artificial territorial divisions and numerical majorities to be a sham and a delusion, and advocated the frank and legal recognition of commerce, industry, property, professions, and crafts in the constitution of the representative system. They held that the doctrine of abstract equality was essentially false and in plain contradiction to the facts of modern social life. They declared that it made the politician a sort of broker (hardly an honest one at that) mediating between conflicting groups and slipping into parliament by deluding electors with phrases, promises, and rhetoric. Thus, in their opinion, the state had passed from the hands of practical and informed men of affairs into the control of the "politicians"—men without any business qualifications whose stock in trade was oratory. Thus they could only see disaster ahead, unless the rhetoricians were expelled and representation restored to the basis of economic realities.

Even more savage in their criticism of numerical democracy and abstract political equality were the socialists. They also declared that the idea of political equality and economic inequality contained an inherent contradiction. They offered, however, a drastic solution—the ownership of all productive property by society and the consequent destruction of both the capitalist class and the working class. The guild socialists, as another school was called, proposed to substitute for the system of numerical and territorial representation a congress composed of delegates from the various craft or trade unions. Still other socialists, fearing the disruptive effects of craft jealousies, insisted that at least one branch of the parliament should represent the people considered as a national unity as distinguished from the people divided into crafts and unions. These last reformers argued that man was a civic and patriotic animal and that his whole nature was not expressed or exhausted in his capacity as an engineer, machinist, or farmer.

All these schemes, however, remained devices on paper until the communist upheaval in Russia in November, 1917. Then the world witnessed the attempt to abolish class antagonisms by the nationalization of land and industrial capital. At the same time the idea of political democracy was denounced and cast aside as a

mere "bourgeois" device calculated to delude the working class. In the place of a congress of representatives
chosen by equal suffrage from territorial districts having substantially the same number of inhabitants, there
was established a soviet or council representing economic groups as such. Whatever may be the outcome
of this upheaval, we must admit that it was a simple and
drastic attempt to dispose of the contradiction between
political theory and economic facts.[2]

The experiment has been carried on long enough for
us now to observe certain general tendencies. The first
is that the nationalization of the land was a mere ges-
ture; the peasants with their feet on the soil remain in
possession of it in spite of parchment and seals. The destruction of the soil-tilling, soil-owning peasant by violence was an utter failure. "Nothing could be more
stupid," said Lenin in March, 1919, "than even the idea
of employing violence against the small owning peasant
class engaged in agricultural exploitation." So the Russian Bolshevists fell back upon a plan of converting the
peasant to communism by showing that co-operative
labor on the land was more productive. At best that
was a millennial undertaking. So the communist order

[2] [The early councils representing workers, peasants, and soldiers
were transitional in nature. Under communist theory all classes, including the proletariat, were to disappear. When the new Russian
constitution was drawn up in 1936 representation in the All-Union
Congress was based on two principles. For one chamber delegates
are apportioned according to population—one delegate per 300,000
inhabitants. In the second chamber, called the Council of Nationalities, the republics constituting the Union are represented. Thus the
Russian constitution of 1936 bears no traces of the class-system such
as appeared in the early councils representing workers, peasants, and
soldiers. See below, p. 77 ff.]

had to reckon with one powerful propertied class.[3]

Without now considering the prophecy that the capitalist class will be restored in Russia under some kind of state socialist design, we may take note of certain tendencies in the working class movement itself. In the first place the operation of the communist system called into being an enormous managerial bureaucracy. According to estimates by Mr. Zinoviev published in July, 1920, approximately one fourth the adults in Petrograd were government officials and another fourth were soldiers. It does not require very much research to discover many signs of conflict and jealousy between the industrial workers and the soft-handed occupants of swivel-chairs.

That is not all. There have been all along conflicts between the craft unions of skilled workers and the communists who were wont to speak of all workers as abstractions, alike and equal. The contention of the communists was of course as great a fiction as the theory of political equality.

When the communists ceased to be mere opponents of capitalists and were charged with management, they soon discovered the unreality of their rhetoric. They likewise discovered the futility of the hope that a system of equality in pay would draw forth vast productive energies. Therefore, they were compelled to negotiate with craft unions and to reward skill and talent with extra remuneration. Of course, they said that this

[3] [At length, however, the communist régime destroyed the class of petty landowners, collectivized agriculture, and "liquidated" recalcitrant peasants. See below, p. 77 ff.]

was all temporary and merely an introduction to the postponed millennium. That may be, but viewing politics from the standpoint of an experimental science, we cannot take into serious account dreams unrealized.

The upshot of all this seems to be·that in a modern industrial society, the problem of property, so vital in politics, is not as simple as it was in old agricultural societies. It was one thing for peasants to destroy their landlords and go on tilling the soil as they had long been wont to do. It is another thing for workingmen to destroy capitalists as a class and assume all the complex and staggering burdens of management and exchange. It is also clear that, as efficient production depends to a great extent upon skill, skill itself is a form of property even if property in capital is abolished.

In short a great society, whether capitalist or communist, must possess different kinds and grades of skill and talent and carry on widely diversified industries. There must be miners, machinists, electricians, engineers, accountants, transport workers, draftsmen, managers, and a hundred other kinds of specialists. They may be temporarily welded together in a conflict with their capitalist employers, but they will be divided over the distribution of wealth among themselves after the capitalists have been disposed of. Conceivably a highly militarist government might destroy their organizations and level them down, but the result would be the ruin of production and of the state itself. Even a communist could hardly defend his system on the theory that all must choose between military despotism and utter ruin.

The grand conclusion, therefore, seems to be exactly that advanced by our own James Madison in the Tenth Number of the Federalist. To express his thought in modern terms: a landed interest, a transport interest, a railway interest, a shipping interest, an engineering interest, a manufacturing interest, a public-official interest, with many lesser interests, grow up of necessity in all great societies and divide them into different classes actuated by different sentiments and views. The regulation of these various and interfering interests, whatever may be the formula for the ownership of property, constitutes the principal task of modern statesmen and involves the spirit of party in the necessary and ordinary operations of government. In other words, there is no rest for mankind, no final solution of eternal contradictions. Such is the design of the universe. The recognition of this fact is the beginning of wisdom—and of statesmanship.

V

Economics and Politics in Our Revolutionary Age

DURING THE PAST QUARTER OF A CENTURY RADICAL changes have occurred in the forms, objects, ownership, management, and rights of property with which economic interests are associated. We no longer live in the simple agricultural era or the simple capitalist era in which the theory of the economic basis of politics was expounded in its starkest form. Nor, for that matter, are we living in a simple communist era as envisaged by the early leaders of the Russian revolution, V. I. Lenin and Leon Trotsky. Rifts and shifts have also taken place in economic thought, both "capitalistic thought" and "communistic thought" as developed in the preceding age.

No less drastic in its consequences has been a transformation in the functions of government, particularly in those which call for wholesale intervention in economic operations. No doubt the nature and course of economy had been more or less shaped and directed by the state from early times. This was especially true under the mercantilist régimes of the seventeenth and eighteenth centuries. But in many western countries during the nineteenth century economic interests enjoyed a high degree of freedom and independence as against the state. In these countries and amid such circumstances it was relatively easy for persons who held property to wield political power. In recent years, however, state intervention in economy has assumed systematic form almost everywhere and the number of persons employed by the state in giving effect to this intervention has greatly multiplied. As a result "the political man" has been gaining in independence from, and in power over, "the economic man" and is now often in a position to order him about rather than to take dictation from him.

Moreover there has been a large-scale revival of belief in, quest for, and exercise of unlimited power in government as an end in itself or as a means to class, national, and imperialistic ends. Power has, of course, always been a characteristic of the state; but in the nineteenth century, with the growth of the middle class and the rise of democracy, it looked for a time as if autocratic authority was everywhere to be controlled by constitutional restraints in the interest of popular welfare and liberty of expression, person, and property. In nations which had made the most effective advances toward constitutional government, such as Great Britain and the United States, it was widely assumed that arbitrary power had been definitely subdued to "the will of the people." Although in other countries at the opening of the twentieth century, for example, Tsarist Russia, Imperial Japan, and Imperial Germany, popular supremacy had not been attained, even there movements in the direction of constitutional government were under way.

When the absolutist order in Russia broke down

during the first World War of our century, efforts were made to erect a constitutional system of government; but they failed, and power was seized by a communist faction under the leadership of a few determined men, notably V. I. Lenin and Leon Trotsky. To this type of power-action a new name was applied—Bolshevism. In sum and substance the philosophy of Bolshevism asserted the right of a small and resolute group to take power "in the name of the proletariat," to set up its own state, and to reduce the rest of the people to obedience.

For this arbitrary seizure and exercise of power the philosophers of Bolshevism, Lenin for instance, had at their command and proclaimed a moral or ideal justification. The dictatorship in the name of the proletariat was to be regarded as temporary, as the forerunner of equality and liberty to come after the state had "withered away." In the ideal order of the future the proletariat as well as every other class was to disappear and "the administration of things" by and for the good of the people was to supplant "the government of men."

In other parts of Europe, after the close of the first World War, the drive for democracy and constitutional government seemed to gain momentum for a period. Constitutions popular in form and containing bills of rights were adopted in Germany, Austria, Yugoslavia, and other European countries, and the suffrage was widened in Japan. But within a few years a reaction occurred, first in Italy. In several countries, governments established by the seizure of power and exercising unlimited power superseded governments checked by popular will and civil liberties.

To this new form of arbitrary power the name of Fascism was generally applied, even to the German type—Nazism. The Fascist state, notwithstanding variations, was the creation of a militant leader and his followers whose authority was sustained by terror and arms, even when some political stratagem was used. By philosophy and action, Fascism repudiated the ideal aims asserted by Bolshevism and likewise the institutions of democracy, constitutionalism, and civil liberty. It exalted and sought to fix permanently the right of a self-chosen élite to rule the rest of the people by the sword and the police. This fact was not and could not be disguised by any of the so-called "corporative constitutions" which Fascism proposed or produced in Italy or Spain.

Although Bolshevism and Fascism differed as to the proclaimed objectives, they agreed in their repudiation of constitutional government as understood in the West. Exponents of both ideologies treated democracy, elections, freedom of the press, and parliamentary politics as a kind of smoke-screen—"a mask for capitalism," to quote Benito Mussolini—devised by the bourgeoisie to conceal its "class dictatorship." In neither system of theory and practice was there any place for government by political majorities victorious at regular elections or for independent courts to uphold civil liberties against attacks by government officials. In short, both unqualifiedly rejected the democratic doctrine of political equality (above, Chapter III). While the Russian communists adopted in 1936 a constitution including a paper program of civil liberties, they were careful to keep sovereign power in the hands of the few—within the communist leadership and the party organization as directed by the supreme leader.

In ways utterly immeasurable and indescribable, two world wars have also altered the social, intellectual, and moral setting in which the theory of the economic basis of politics was discussed prior to 1914. From Aristotle's time down through the centuries the theory had been limited by the condition that economic forces operate freely only in the absence of military force (above, pp. 9, 12, 21 ff., 29, 55); but during the long period between the close of the Napoleonic wars in 1815 and the opening of the first World War in 1914, the conditional clause, which severely limited the theory, had been regarded as largely academic, particularly in the United States. Now a single generation has experienced the shattering impacts of military force around the globe on a scale beyond all precedents. Not an aspect of life—economic, political, intellectual or emotional— has escaped its actions and devastations. During the momentous years since 1914 "the military man" has again entered into full competition with "the economic man" and "the political man" for power over the state and its fortunes.

Events in Russia since 1917 especially demand a reconsideration of the economic basis of politics as made manifest under Bolshevism and Communism. In old communist theory the idea of economic determinism in politics assumed a definite form: hitherto all history had been the history of class struggles; after the establishment of the communist society classes will disappear; humanity will spring into freedom; long the victim of economic forces and conflicts, humanity will become master over them. Between this closing of old history and the opening of the era of perpetual liberty and universal welfare, the dictatorship of power in the name of the proletariat was, according to the theory, to be regarded as a mere transitory episode, perhaps painful, but necessary to attain the desired goal. In the light of recent events in Russia, how does the communist conception of the economic basis of politics stand up?

What would have happened if Lenin had lived ten or fifteen years longer, no one knows. The Russian revolution might have taken another turn. But at any rate after his death it pursued the classical course so common in revolutions: a struggle for dominance ensued among his most eminent subordinates; by one process of liquidation or another the number of contestants for supreme leadership was materially reduced. Leon Trotsky was exiled, and later murdered in Mexico. At length Joseph Stalin emerged as dictator, supported by the police and the sword.

For a time it seemed as if the Stalin régime was dedicated particularly to the realization of "socialism in one country." But Russia's experiences with the Western governments during the early stage of the Bolshevik revolution warned her officials to be vigilant in building up her military defenses. The approach of war and then the coming of war forced an enormous and strict militarization of Russian economy. Stalin's extraordinary successes in diplomacy and warfare, coupled with the rise of a new military class, strengthened his system of power. Meanwhile a transformation of Russian society was going forward.

What had appeared in 1919 to be an insuperable obstacle to a complete nationalization of agriculture (above, p. 67)—the tenacity with which the small peasants clung to their lands—was finally overcome, subject to minor concessions. Lenin had opposed the use of violence against the peasant. After he died, however, the Soviet government adopted a policy of extreme land nationalization and carried it out by forcible methods—including the "liquidation" and deportation of recalcitrant peasants by the millions. Thus a propertied class numerically large was exterminated, and communism, or collectivization, was established even in agriculture.[1] By 1939 the small landowners of the old régime had gone the way of the great landlords, bureaucrats, and middle classes of the Tsarist days. Former class barriers had been levelled.

According to communist theory Russia was now supposed to be "classless," for the distinctions founded on landed and other forms of material property had been extinguished, at least as far as direct ownership was concerned. But other important kinds of social dis-

[1] "In 1940 almost all the agricultural production in the [Soviet] Union came from the 240,000 consolidated collective farms that had taken the place of the 25,000,000 separate peasant holdings that had existed in 1928." B. H. Sumner, *A Short History of Russia* (1943), p. 115. Only a certain number of animals, small implements, and gardens are now individually owned but this branch of private enterprise is highly productive.

tinction rapidly developed. The introduction of technology into socialized agriculture was attended by gradations of technical competence among the millions nominally called "workers on the land." In connection with this transformation appeared large numbers of agronomists, engineers, skilled farm mechanics, managers, bookkeepers, specialists in plant and animal husbandry, and other sorts of experts. Moreover in the train of the vast industrialization came a differentiation of urban occupations and callings almost as complicated and hierarchical as those to be found in the capitalistic societies of the West: engineers and managers of all kinds, plant foremen, and a classified personnel ranging from skilled machine operatives at the apex to untrained casual laborers at the bottom.

To plan, coordinate, direct, and govern the huge economic and political aggregations of the Russian Union an immense bureaucracy was evolved. It was graded from the over-all executives at the top down through various territorial and specialized officials to the petty functionaries at the lowest rung of the ladder. Amid the exigencies of military preparations and war, an armed force of gigantic proportions was created and it also had its graded personnel ranging from the chief of staff down to non-commissioned officers and regimented men.

In the civil and foreign wars which immediately followed the Bolshevik revolution of 1917, Soviet authorities had been compelled to rely upon improvisation—mainly upon the selection of military leaders from among the rank and file of soldiers and, indeed, from among civilians. The spectacular military performances of Trotsky as an amateur, in the period of the civil warfare, illustrates this point. But as time passed, more and more reliance was placed on men professionally trained for war and provisions were made for their training. Thus a large body of professional military officers came into being, with a corresponding system of military education, selection, promotion, distinctions in rank, and esprit de corps. Unlike the officer class of Prussian Junkers, whose landed property gave them a certain degree of economic independence as against the state, the new Russian officer class was wholly dependent upon the state for its emoluments, prestige, and distinctions.

If, after years of such developments, the post-revolutionary Russian society was still nominally classless, in the sense that there were no longer classes based on the ownership of land and other productive property, it was in fact a highly differentiated society, with great divergencies in power, security, and income. If there were no propertied classes, there were income-classes, and classes with favored positions in respect of advancement and economic advantages. As the differentiation proceeded, a tendency to stratification appeared, first in fact and then more slowly in law. This process was quickened by an early abandonment of the communist formula: "from each according to his ability and to each according to his needs," and the substitution of "incentive pay" for industrial workers and graded salaries for members of the civil and military bureaucracy.

As a consequence of the larger incomes for members

of the upper grades of workers in industries and for members of the higher civil and military bureaucracy, millions of Russians were able to accumulate money for personal expenditures or for deposit in savings banks or investment in government bonds. If nominally on the same footing as other Russian citizens, these recipients of higher incomes formed a substantial portion of the population differentiated from their less fortunate neighbors in the matter of claims to personal property and goods. The children of these people possessed privileges denied to the offspring of less favored families: privileges of leisure, comfort, convenience, and education, helpful in the gratification of tastes and ambitions. Such children could be better prepared for passing entrance examinations to the institutions of higher learning that trained youth for the civil and military professions and for occupations in the upper ranges of industry and the bureaucracy. After graduation they could call on powerful friends for help in securing lucrative positions in economic hierarchy.

In this course of affairs, the family, treated by many of the early Bolsheviks as a moribund "bourgeois" institution, was gradually brought back into the history from which they had sought to expel it. Russian laws accelerated the restoration: for example, legislation relative to inheritance, marriage, maternal subsidies, divorce, and abortion. It is true that Russia was not reviving landed, industrial, and financial families of the old style. But Russia was reconstituting the family as an economic, cultural, and social institution, with all that this implied in terms of marked differentiations in society. By intermarriage among members of the upper-income families, family ties and family influences in economy, education, and the struggle for position were reinforced.[2]

These tendencies in Russian society did not signify, as some American innocents abroad liked to imagine, a return to historic capitalism or "free enterprise." They did indicate, however, that the communist ideal of free and equal individuals, having identical economic opportunities, having no special privileges of income and position, was not being realized. It also meant that, however "classless" Russian society might now be in theory, it had in truth highly differentiated and graded economic interests which were recognized by government and law. Moreover it meant that as such interests grew in vigor, they were bound to find expression in the thinking, the ideology, and, more or less, in the politics of the country.

Ten years after the revolution of 1917 a stratification

[2] From the standpoint of those old Bolsheviks who regarded the family as a form of bourgeois servitude to be abolished in favor of sex liberty, the most revolutionary piece of Soviet legislation in respect of the family is the Act of July 8, 1944, providing subsidies and special monthly pensions for mothers, graded in amount according to the number of their children. The Act also grants other special privileges to mothers, accords special protection to them and their children, creates medals and orders of maternity, imposes special taxes on childless and small families, and makes modifications in the former laws relative to matrimony, the family, and guardianship. A Spanish translation of this Act appears in *Boletín de Información* (Legation of the Soviet Union at Havana) for February 5, 1945. This number also contains valuable articles on the Russian family. One of the most interesting of these articles is entitled *La Familia Sovietica, Escuela de Patriotismo*, pp. 8–9. For criticism of the libertarian theories in respect of marriage during the early years of the Revolution, see pp. 10–11.

of the Russian communist society had already become marked. In 1927, when the Communist Party claimed approximately 1,200,000 members, about 600,000 were officials and bureaucratic employees of the government, as against 150,000 workers on the land and 450,-000 workers in factories. These officials and bureaucratic employees had accumulated considerable personal property. According to the figures for 1930, individual deposits in savings banks amounted to 476,-000,000 rubles (apart from the deposits of cooperatives and collectives); and of this total, officials and bureaucratic employees held 205,000,000 rubles, while laborers held 90,000,000 rubles, and peasants held the balance.[3] In three years, between 1925 and 1928, the number of holders of internal loan bonds in Soviet Russia increased from 100,000 to 10,000,000.[4] Exact figures for later dates are not available but it is estimated that in 1939 more than 50,000,000 people were holders of state bonds, and that at the end of 1944 internal bonds to the amount of 117,200,000,000 rubles were outstanding.[5] At the beginning of 1940 at least 37,000 savings banks were in operation and had on deposit a little more than 7,000,000,000 rubles. The total number of de-

[3] A. Rosenberg, *Geschichte des Bolschewismus*, pp. 193, 229.
[4] A. Willehn (Alfred H. Vagts), "Internationale Finanz und internationale Politik," Europaische Gespräche, October, 1928, p. 514, note.
[5] From the total outstanding debt should be deducted gifts of bonds to the state by private citizens. These gifts have been large. In 1944 it was announced that gifts of state bonds to the amount of 4 billion rubles had been made to the Red Army Fund. But figures for the total amount of gifts do not seem to be available in the United States at the beginning of the year 1945.

positors was then placed at 16,802,000 as compared with 15,547,000 in 1939.[6]

The statistical publications of Soviet Russia, at least those now available in the United States, provide little or no information about gradations in income-groups. They certainly do not permit the presentation of an exact picture showing (1) all the various occupational groups and the exact number of persons in each group; (2) a classification of the Russian population according to incomes and the number of persons in each income-bracket (such as may be found in the official statistics of the United States); and (3) a classification of population according to holdings of property, such as household goods, government bonds, savings deposits, land and livestock allotments, authors' royalty rights, and so forth.

But Russian official documents do indicate that Russian society is divided into a number of classes, each consisting of individuals receiving incomes within a certain range, and all graded from low levels of income upwards to annual salaries of 24,000 rubles and more per year. Though the Soviet Government apparently does not make available the exact number of persons in each income category, the fact of the income-categories is recognized and used in the tax legislation (Old

[6] Among the sources for more recent figures on the Russian debt and savings bank deposits are: U. S. Department of Commerce, Internal Debt Compiled from Announcements of Loans in Russian Newspapers by E. C. Ropes; U. S. Department of Commerce, Russian Economic Notes, March 15, 1940; the *American Review of the Soviet Union*, June, 1941; *Soviet Information Bulletin*, September 29, 1944.

Income Tax, 1940 rates; Housing and Cultural Tax, 1940 rates; and War Income Tax of December 29, 1941).

Special evidence bearing on the stratification of Russian society comes from reports on the tax and revenue system of the Soviet government. That system reflects and in some respects accentuates the gradations in Russian economy. It is not wholly grounded on the simple equalitarian principle that the tax laid on each person should be exactly adjusted to his income or ability to pay. In other words, the nature and rates of taxation in Soviet Russia are not such as to make the members of the various income groups carry tax burdens apportioned strictly and progressively according to their respective abilities in terms of wealth.

On this point we have recent information from Dr. Jerome Davis, a sympathetic and observant student of Russian institutions.[7] The largest single source of revenue for the Soviet state, he says, is "the turnover tax." Far less important as a revenue producer is the war income tax. Dr. Davis says that annual income up to 1,800 rubles is taxable to the amount of 120 rubles. The tax rate rises but apparently levels off at incomes of 24,000 rubles; it is 1,020 rubles on incomes between 9,600 and 10,800 rubles; and it is 2,700 rubles on incomes above 24,000 rubles. On farmers, it ranges from 150 to 500 rubles a year. There are, of course, various exemptions. Voluntary donations and lotteries afford substantial revenues. Another source is state loans. At the outset of the war in 1941 the state debt was about

[7] *The New Republic*, January 1, 1945 (cabled from Moscow).

50,000,000,000 rubles; three war loans of 1942, 1943, and 1944 brought in around 61,000,000,000 rubles.

Official reports and other publications issued under the auspices of the Soviet Government or with its authorization permit, therefore, a classification of the Russian people on the basis of power, culture, and/or income, which often corresponds more or less closely to positions in the hierarchy. Exact figures are lacking, but the following general picture as of 1944 is based on a substantial documentation:

I. High officials in the Communist party. The party membership is about 5,000,000. High officials in the party are often high officials in the Soviet Government on its political side and on its economic side.

II. High officials and intellectuals in Russian society, inside and outside the Communist Party, often with relatively high incomes, especially those in posts of industrial management and those engaged in writing, editing, and propaganda.

III. Minor officials of the white collar class, numbering millions: engineers, technicians, statisticians, economists, bookkeepers, chauffeurs, mechanics, teachers, police, and so forth.

IV. Industrial workers of many types, crafts, and skills. Their number is variously estimated at from one-fifth of the population upwards.

V. Workers on the land (peasants) comprising about one half of the population. The amount of time given by the land worker to labor on state farms and the amount given to the cultivation of his own allotment varies from place to place and time to time.

VI. Forced labor. Composed of prisoners of one kind or another scattered about the country in labor camps. Exact number unknown. Sometimes estimated in the millions.

If long experiences in other ages and places are any guide in making forecasts, certain things are likely to happen in Russia during the coming years. As James Madison might put the case, these strong and often conflicting interests will perdure and provide substance and force in Russian politics in the future. Should Russia enter into a long era of peace, the more powerful among these interests could scarcely fail to seek representation and force in government, if not control over the state. Should the military interest become supreme in the decades ahead, it would subdue civilian interests to its will, perhaps for a long period of time. For, as Daniel Webster's axiom runs, it is only in the absence of the sword that economic interests may rule (above, p. 21).

With military interests, foreign as well as domestic politics comes into consideration. No military body whose directors are recruited largely from an officer, or military, class can easily maintain itself in power, if at all, without wars and rumors of war. Historically, Russia had been one of the great warlike nations of Europe during more than a century prior to the Bolshevik revolution of 1917. For a time, and partly owing to its internal weakness at first, Bolshevik Russia renounced imperialism and under compulsion surrendered large areas of the country to her neighbors. To some extent this repudiation of imperialism was due to the hope of idealists that workers' revolutions would occur all over Europe and lead to a federation of communist republics. But after 1939, and particularly after the sensational victories over the Germans in the sec-

ond World War, Russian leadership seemed to renew
the territorial and power ambitions of Tsarist Russia.

As everyone knows who has even an elementary ac-
quaintance with Russian history since the age of Peter
the Great, Russian territorial and power ambitions have
contemplated a wide sweep in Europe and Asia and
have been accompanied by the rise and growth of Pan-
Slavism. That Russian military planning and education
will take these traditions into account, for strategic
studies, preparations, and calculations of actions, is
practically certain. Nor will the upper levels of the
civilian bureaucracy be indifferent to the advantages
that may be derived from economic and other forms of
penetration into regions around the borders of the great
Soviet Union. And here a peculiar factor may come into
service. Unlike the interests behind the imperialist expansion of Western countries, Russian interests are
vitalized by ideological ties with revolutionary parties
in other areas, near and distant; they may profit by, if
they do not foment, disturbances that will lead to intervention in a manner that resembles imperialistic action
but may be defended on "moral" grounds.

Notwithstanding variations in the types of Fascism,
particularly in "racist" theories and practices, the political and economic formulas and actions of Fascism
were substantially identical wherever it appeared. The
leader, supported by armed bands, was the head of the
state—indeed the state itself; and the institutions associated with constitutional government and civil liberty
were suppressed. All property was not taken over by

the Fascist state, as it had been in Russia. Nor were the upper, middle, and farming classes liquidated. But the uses of property and the enjoyment of fruits and profits from property were so restricted as to destroy innumerable rights of persons in property as historically understood and defined.

It is true that the Weimar constitution designed for a republic in Germany after the first World War was not formally and entirely discarded by the Nazis. Yet for all practical purposes it was abolished. In Italy some efforts were made to give a voice in government to corporations, that is, to grant representation to specific organized classes—managerial, industrial, and commercial for example—but these classes were denied all power of free choice in the selection of their agents. It was alleged in Italy that the goal of Fascism was the creation of "the corporative state," reproducing in a modern form something like the class hierarchy of estates in the middle ages. No such end was actually achieved, however. State power under Fascism in Italy as well as elsewhere remained absolutely independent of the people considered as political or economic individuals or as members of private associations. Economic interests of all kinds were in theory, and to a large extent in practice, subdued to the will of the state— namely, to the dictator, checked if at all only by the advice of his party council. Protests were smothered by the police.

Many attempts have been made to explain the rise and growth of the Fascist state in terms almost purely economic, as if the Fascist dictator and his colleagues were the mere automata of interests called "capital-istic." It has been claimed that Fascism was the logical and inevitable answer of sheer capitalist power to the menace of sheer communist power. Another explanation is to the effect that Fascism was simply the product of the unemployment, poverty, and social unrest which came in the wake of the first World War—economic distresses with which democratic and parliamentary governments could not cope. A communist formula of explanation declares that Fascism is the last stage of exploitive capitalism and is to be succeeded by the final revolutionary triumph of the industrial proletariat under the banner of communism.

In the name of free enterprise or laissez-faire capital-ism another economic explanation of Fascism has been offered; for instance, in F. A. Hayek's *The Road to Serfdom.* According to this thesis "the rise of Fascism and Nazism was not a reaction against the socialist trends of the preceding period but a necessary outcome of these tendencies." In other words, Fascism, in its German and Italian expression and in incipient expres-sions elsewhere, was due to the abandonment of the individualist tradition, the growth of capitalistic mo-nopolies, the suppression of free competition, and the adoption of state intervention or planning in economy. Thus the Western democracies, as well as other coun-tries, are on the road that leads to Fascist serfdom, for they have adopted protective tariffs, planning, and other types of state interference with the old "natural order of things" in which the competition of individuals prevailed. Here no distinction is made between state

intervention by despotisms and state intervention by
constitutional governments under popular mandates.
Intervention in economy *per se* leads to Fascism.

Certainly economic interests figured in the rise and
growth of Fascism. There were grave economic disturbances in Italy when Mussolini came to power in
that country and undoubtedly the great depression in
Germany made it easier for Hitler to seize the state
in 1933. Unquestionably both Mussolini and Hitler appealed to industrial workers, peasants, and the lower
middle classes as against the rich and the insurgent
communists. Hitler practically promised "the people"
everything they thought they wanted. Indisputably the
two rising dictators received monetary aid from large
financial and industrial interests. In both countries, perhaps more in Italy than in Germany, big industrialists
were often granted special favors at the expense of the
lower middle and laboring classes.

But purely economic interpretations of the rise,
growth, and nature of Fascism are oversimplifications.
They rest upon a theory of the economic basis of politics unqualified by the condition attached to it by the
keenest thinkers who made use of it—the condition that
only in the absence of military force does political
power pass into the hands of those who hold the property (above, p. 21 ff.). This is to say that oversim-
plified economic interpretations treat economic interests as if they are always and everywhere independent
"causes" of political actions and institutions; as if they
universally furnish the most powerful if not the sole
impetus to political action for the conquest of power

in the state, in times of war, civil and foreign, as well as in times of peace.

Economic explanations pure and simple leave out of the reckoning other aspects of human motivation; for instance, the ambitions and force of unique personalities; the spirit of resentment in Italy over the curt treatment received at Versailles in 1919; and the passion for revenge in Germany after defeat in the first World War. They ignore the role played in Fascism by those soldiers of that war who were still filled with passion for destroying, killing, and dominating. Nor must it be forgotten that the elements of Fascist ideology had long been awaiting use by activists in search of adventure and power in the war-torn world. Among these elements were the racial doctrines of Count Gobineau and H. S. Chamberlain; anti-semitic diatribes; virulent abuse of "democracy" and "civilization"; exaltations of irrationality and violence as masculine virtues; and the systematic formulations of Sorel, Mosca, and Pareto in criticism of the masses and popular government. Economic forces undoubtedly entered into the rise of Fascism but they do not wholly account for its appearance and course.

In the United States during the past twenty-five years modifications in interests and ideas pertinent to the economic basis of politics and additions to knowledge of the subject warrant a review and restatement of the theory. The forms and relationships of economic and political realities have been altered in many fundamental respects. Economists of the institutional school and statisticians have furnished more minute descriptions of economic practices, processes, and tendencies. Careful studies of voting habits and of contributions to campaign funds for use in elections have revealed in descriptive and mathematical terms various connections and correlations between economic interests and party affiliations.

By general agreement it had been early recognized that the great manufacturing and financial interests in the country were, in the main, on the Republican side of the political alignment. There were exceptions, of course, especially among manufacturers and financiers whose fortunes depended largely on export and import business and in the South where political attachments were nominally Democratic for special reasons. But on the whole the major manufacturing and financial interests were Republican, with all that signified in terms of protective tariffs, taxation, banking, government promotion of private enterprise, non-intervention in "the natural distribution of wealth," and laissez faire in many forms. And despite concessions to progressive and radical factions, the Republicans hewed rather close to the party line from 1921 to 1929, the period of so-called Republican prosperity.

At all events during that period (1921–1929), manufacturing and financial interests enjoyed a high degree of prosperity. There was some unemployment among industrial workers but the amount was not large enough to produce wholesale disaffection in their ranks. Only among farmers was there widespread economic distress. Although that distress made itself felt in politics, it was not strong enough to bring about a political overturn. Thus, Republican politics had a fairly secure economic basis during those years, while Democrats wandered in the political desert. Had their economic basis continued to be firm, Republicans might well have enjoyed an indefinite tenure of power. The election returns for 1928 certainly pointed in that direction.

In 1929, however, "prosperity" went to pieces. How far that crash was due to Republican policies, whether it could have been avoided by Democratic politicians had they been in power, and similar questions of "causation" are issues which simply cannot be resolved by any kind of analysis, economic, political, or historical. But according to the scapegoat axiom of politics, the Republicans, who had claimed credit for the prosperity, were discredited by the depression, poverty, and unemployment which followed the crack of 1929, and in the election of 1932 they were swept out of office in an avalanche of votes.

This is not to argue that the voters in 1932 were convinced that the Democrats could or would restore "prosperity," or provide a degree of economic well-being sufficient to allay the political unrest which sprang from the depression. Nor is there warrant for claiming that in the campaign of 1932 the Democrats presented a clear outline of just what they intended to do in the way of "restoring," "recovering," or "creating" prosperity. In fact, apart from introducing various measures of regulation and social security long overdue, the Democrats, under President Franklin D. Roosevelt's leadership, failed to overcome the depression by the policies they put into effect in his first administration. In 1938 the number of unemployed workers was at least three times the number recorded during the peak months of "prosperity" under President Calvin Coolidge. It was not until the boom created by preparations for war and the still greater boom created by the war itself that Democratic politics achieved a temporary "prosperity" almost nation-wide in its range.

In the meantime, while the Democrats at the national capital were wrestling with the dislocations in economy and trying to get it into a higher speed of production, politics was gaining in power over economics. In part this gain represented a continuation of old tendencies but in a larger part it was marked by so much novelty that it could be characterized, with some justification, as revolutionary in upshot if not in purpose. In any case drastic shifts were effected in the methods of politics and in the economic basis of politics. Of these shifts only a few can be listed here, as illustrative.

At the head of the list belong the adoption and execution of the policy of *large-scale taxing, borrowing, and spending for many purposes under government, or political, auspices.*

Among the purposes were: to stimulate and promote private enterprise in industry and agriculture; to increase the amount of employment; to provide economic security for millions of dependent persons; to make preparations for war; and to wage war, after 1941.

It is true that for some of these operations there were precedents. When the panic broke in 1929 President

Herbert Hoover urged the expansion of federal spending for public works and called upon the states to follow the federal example; and in other ways federal money and credit were used during the Hoover administration in aid of private enterprise and home loan institutions. But the degree of federal taxing, borrowing, and spending after 1933 reached such a height as to constitute an economic overturn, far-reaching in its consequences.

By numerous and complicated measures, sometimes connected with the policy of taxing and spending and sometimes standing alone, *manufacturing, commercial, financial, and agricultural interests, once treated as primarily private and as forming the chief economic basis of politics, were made dependent upon politics to an extent which in this respect signalized a breach with the past.*

To describe the new network of relationships would require a monumental treatise. Whole segments of industry, business, and agriculture now rely heavily upon government spending, for civilian and war purposes, as a main source of the popular buying power that keeps economy in motion and prosperity. Having lost their gold coins and bullion to the Federal Government and having filled their vaults with federal bonds and other paper, bankers have become in a large measure mere agents of the Government in Washington. No longer do these powerful interests stand, so to speak, "outside the Government" and in a position to control or dictate to it; all of them are closely linked in their fortunes to the fortunes of politics.

This must not be taken to imply, of course, that the powerful industrial and financial interests of the United States have been expropriated according to the formula of Marxian, as distinguished from American, Communists or that they have become the mere servants of "political men." Far from it. The saying current in 1933 that the New Deal had saved frightened capitalists from a destructive revolution expressed a conviction then and still held by many Democrats high in the councils of the party. Furthermore, since 1933 numerous friends and patrons of the New Deal have complained that great capitalists have been all along entrenched in the strategic centers of the Roosevelt administrations. The controversy in 1945 over the selection of certain assistants as aides to the Secretary of State, Edward Stettinius, himself a former associate of the powerful Morgan interests, turned in part on this very point. So did the dispute about the ousting of Jesse Jones from the direction of federal lending agencies and the appointment of Henry Wallace as Secretary of Commerce.

With regard to the alleged power of big capitalists in the Roosevelt administrations two other facts have pertinence. The long list of capitalist contributors to the Republican campaign funds for the elections of 1936, 1940, and 1944 indicates that the amount of power exercised by capitalists in the Federal Government was not sufficient to meet their own conceptions of their interests in innumerable cases. Still more significant in this relation is the fact that capitalism, free enterprise, and "trust-busting" somewhat in the economic style of William Jennings Bryan in 1896 were supported by the very left-wing of the New Dealers headed by Henry Wallace, endorsed by leaders in the Political Action Committee of the Congress of Industrial Organizations, and approved, temporarily at least, by American Communists of the Stalin school. The expropriation of capitalists in favor of "political men" formed no part of the New Deal program as of 1945. Nevertheless in that year industrial and financial interests did not have any such independent power in politics as they had exercised in 1928 or 1916 or 1900.

During the evolution of the New Deal, another large interest, formerly regarded as essentially private, has assumed a semi-political and semi-official character. *Fourteen or fifteen million industrial and white collar workers organized in trades and general unions have acquired a special position in law and have thus attached their fortunes to the fortunes of politics.* To consolidate and fortify this attachment one of the national federations of labor—the Congress of Industrial Organizations—established the Committee for Political Action in 1944 and, with no little reason, claimed to have assured the re-election of President Roosevelt in that year.

Nominally as yet, organized labor possesses a high degree of independence. But some of its privileges have been won by political instead of economic action; and it has entrusted the supervision of important elections and decisions in union affairs to federal agencies, thus regularly invoking the intervention and protection of the Government directly in behalf of its interests. To this extent it has become entangled in the vicissitudes of politics and the state. Although organized labor had participated in campaigns and elections in limited ways for more than half a century, the degree and nature of its participation in 1944 indicated that it had reached a new stage in its relations to government and politics, and had made a deeper plunge into the opposition of interests that provides dynamics for politics, especially where freedom of opinion and elections is practiced.

To carry out New Deal policies in general and particular, *an enormous body of public officials and employees, Federal and state, has been added to the older and relatively small bureaucracy.* In other words, while the number of private citizens and concerns enjoying direct benefits from government expenditures increased, the apparatus of government, central and local, reached proportions never before attained in the United States. Now the political party in power has a huge army of office-holders dependent upon it for jobs, emoluments, promotion, and prestige, and hence by interest inclined to keep it indefinitely in all places of political authority.

Late in 1944 the United States Bureau of the Census reported that the Federal Government had 3,335,000 civil employees, and that state and local governments had 3,168,000, making a total of 6,503,000 public functionaries. Estimating the number of inhabitants at 138,-100,875, the Census Bureau reckoned the number of place-holders at nearly one in twenty of the population. Since each place-holder usually has one or more family relatives, frequently dependents, it becomes evident that this class, whose fortunes are directly attached to those of government, is in a position to wield immense power in politics and society. It is true that in 1944 about two million of the civil employees were in government places connected with the war and that in time many of them may or will be returned to private life. But even so, the number of place-holders will remain large enough to exercise a decisive influence in close elections under the rule of political equality— "one person, one vote." Hence it must be recorded that a new kind of class has appeared in America: a large and permanent bureaucracy composed of political men and women whose economic support is derived mainly if not wholly from politics.

Under the policies of taxing, spending, regulating, and promoting, politicians have put a special sort of floor under their operating machine. Millions of farmers, industrialists, industrial workers, and government employees are made directly dependent upon government actions, that is, politics, for part or all of their profits, wages or other income. Millions of aged and dependent persons are henceforward to obtain all or a substantial portion of their economic support from government, central or local or both in cooperation. Until the war-boom demand for labor exceeded the supply, millions of unemployed persons turned to the Federal Government in search of employment or relief; but the boom is admittedly temporary. An end to such prosperity is inevitable.

The political party phase of the economic shifts is patent. In former times party organizations had been maintained principally by contributions from private economic interests desirous of government favors. With funds derived from such sources, party managers carried on campaigns and employed many devices in influencing voters. But under the new régime Democratic politicians, while continuing old ways of collecting party funds, merely have to remind a multitude of voters that they depend directly and immediately upon politics for innumerable tangible benefits received. Indeed it is likely that few of these voters need to be reminded of anything so daily obvious to them. Once Republican politicians had overtly called the attention of manufacturers to the benefits derived from Republican tariff policies; but the number of voters immediately represented by such interests was relatively small. Now the number of voters receiving economic returns from politics mounts upwards into the tens of millions.

Despite all the changes which have taken place in economics and politics during the past quarter of a century, the democratic theory of free and equal heads still rules in American politics, for the most part (see above, Chapter III). Tax and other qualifications on the suffrage in general and special discriminations against Negroes in many states offer contradictions but the proportion of the adult population that can and does vote is very large. And in practice party divisions show a high degree of correlation with divisions into income groups. By numerous polls taken during election campaigns, notably since 1936, evidence has been furnished to the effect that *the major portion of the Democratic voters belong to the lower income-groups and that the major portion of the voters in the upper income-groups are to be found in the Republican column.* Thus modern research and polling methods have developed statistical support for the theory of the economic basis of politics formulated by James Madison in 1787 (above, pp. 16–19).

While "the political man" has been gaining in authority over "the economic man," American foreign policies and wars since 1898 have rendered necessary the enlargement of military interests in economy and politics. The significance of this development must be appreciated in any effort to understand the tendencies of our times; for it leads to the expectation that *"the military man"* and *"military force"* *will play an increasing role in the public affairs of the United States* as well as in the affairs of other countries.

This outcome of recent war experiences was not wholly unforeseen. For many years advocates of internationalism have insisted that "nationalism" and "isolationism," as well as "imperialism," require a huge military and naval establishment—"militarism," in short; and that only by a system of collective security on a world scale can this menace to civilian life and civilian government, including the burdensome cost, be avoided.

Arguments of the kind were prominent in the debate over the League of Nations at the close of the first World War and provisions were made in the Versailles treaty for a reduction of armaments. Although the United States took part in the general conference on that subject, no agreement on reductions could be reached by the great Powers. Again, before and after the United States became involved in the second World War, similar arguments respecting the dangers of militarism were advanced in favor of American participation in the war and in a permanent union of nations to prevent militarism.

However, early in 1945, after victory over Germany and Japan seemed assured and American membership in an organization of nations for collective security appeared almost certain, a demand arose in the United States for an extensive program of armaments, including universal military service, to be put into effect after the war as a permanent national system. In his message to Congress on January 6, 1945, President Roosevelt declared himself in favor of making universal training a regular feature of American military policy after peace was restored. It is true that he insisted on the creation of an international organization for collective security, but he evidently did not deem the achievement of that design a sufficient guarantee for the protection of the United States against foreign dangers.

If the new policy is adopted, then the United States will have a gigantic military and naval establishment, modelled more or less on similar institutions long maintained by the great Powers of the world. That will be followed by an immense growth in the number of persons, especially officers, devoted entirely to the occupations of the armed services. This is not to contend that military men are more warlike than civilians; often they are in fact less warlike. But military men have, necessarily, a set of values which differ in many respects from civilian values; and the military interests, enlarged by universal conscription, will constitute a powerful influence in American affairs, with all that may involve amid the domestic and foreign contingencies of coming ages.

A RECONSIDERATION OF THE ECONOMIC THESIS

In reconsidering an idea as deeply entangled in powerful interests as the idea of the economic basis of politics, no person can hope to be wholly "disinterested," wholly detached and Olympian. He may strive to follow the example of Descartes and put preconceptions out of his mind, but he is almost certain to find them returning, perhaps by the "back-door," as Descartes did. We are not under obligations to accept the associational psychology of John Locke as the whole truth; yet we are all, in some measure, victims of ideas derived from our experiences and associations.

There are few, if any, ideas relative to human affairs which all men and women of every class, clime, race, nation, and age can look upon coldly and agree upon as readily as they can upon the proposition that the circumference of a circle is equal to 3.1416 times its diameter, approximately. Certainly the proposition that "in the absence of military force, political power naturally and necessarily goes into the hands which hold the property" is not a statement likely to be viewed with chill detachment and universally accepted, defended, or criticized without emotion.

Even so, this does not imply that we may not with some success seek the utmost truth about particular aspects of human affairs in detail and in general. Indeed by an informed awareness of relevant preconceptions—sectarian, partisan, and factional, including our own —we may to some extent rise above them or shake off their tyranny. At all events, the theory of the economic basis of politics may be more effectively reconsidered if these admonitions are kept in mind.

Although this theory is ancient in origin, the modern statement of it was formulated in particular circumstances and on the basis of assumptions connected with those circumstances. It was in England and the United States that the thesis was earliest promulgated in comprehensive form and applied to practical politics. And in England civilian supremacy over the monarchy and army was attained by the end of the seventeenth century; in the United States civilian supremacy over all armed forces was guaranteed by the Constitution which went into effect in 1789.

The geographical position of these two countries, given the state of war technology, made unnecessary the maintenance of huge armies for purposes of offense or defense. While high standing was accorded to the military man in both nations, military virtues were subordinated to civilian virtues—in economic terms, industrial, commercial, and agricultural virtues. In England and the United States, from the latter part of the eighteenth century onward, constitutional government, with emphasis on civil liberties, generally prevailed; thus conditions favored the easy expression of economic interests in politics, and the exercise of power by such interests in affairs of state. Upon the assumption that these conditions would continue indefinitely, politics was extensively treated as if the theory of the economic basis of politics supplied the criteria for "explaining" politics always and everywhere.

It should also be remembered that Karl Marx, who reduced all history to class struggles and formulated the theory of materialist determinism near the middle of the nineteenth century, conducted his major economic studies in England and used English capitalism as the classical example. It is true that Marx and his collaborator, Friedrich Engels, gave some attention to war as a social phenomenon; but neither of them substantially qualified his "economic man" by reference to the role of the military man in universal history. In fact Marx built his system largely on Manchester economics and then evolved his own theory of social dynamics, known as dialectical materialism. It may be truly said that in some ways he was a victim of capitalistic theories then in vogue and of Hegelian metaphysics.

The general conception of Manchesterism as applied to universal history was, up to a certain point, almost identical with that of Marxism. Capitalism was bound to spread throughout the world, reaching at length the most remote and backward places. Old military societies were to be transformed into industrial societies. "The economic man" would completely subdue "the military man," the state would shrink, and the administration of things for human welfare would take the place of government by force. Manchesterism saw this occurring as the area of capitalistic laissez faire was extended and as free trade among nations was progressively realized; and Marx introduced a proletarian revolution as a prelude to universal liberty and well-being. But both systems of historical interpretation looked forward to world peace, economic prosperity, and the decline, if not the disappearance, of "the military man" and the state. Even Marx himself thought that the socialist transformation might be effected in England and the United States by constitutional as distinguished from violent methods.

Nevertheless the prophecies of Manchesterism and Marxism have not been realized. The whole world has not been fully industrialized or turned to the peaceful pursuits of economic production. In recent years the area of the earth occupied by constitutional and democratic governments has diminished rather than increased. The multitude of people living under the sword of empires and under dictatorial states maintained by military force outnumbers by far the multitude living under systems of government which allow a high degree of economic and political liberty. "The political man" and "the military man" have gained at the expense of "the economic man." The state has not withered away, as communists once confidently predicted, even under communism as enforced in Russia. Calculations respecting the future of both economic and political forces must still be balanced by calculations as to the possible weight of sheer power and the sword in the years ahead.

Yet amid recent changes one thing remains certain. Politics, including military aspects, must have an economic basis or perish. People must have food, clothing, and shelter before and while they engage in politics and fighting. Whatever the formulas for the ownership and use of property, the state—despotic or democratic—must secure for itself an economic underwriting sufficient to sustain it or it will in fact wither away, as many states and empires have in the past. "The man of war," with his insatiable demand for materials, is even more than ever dependent upon economic production and, if he strives for political sovereignty, he must make sure that an adequate economic underpinning is provided or he will be destroyed by his own works. It is in these circumstances and subject to such qualifications that the economic basis of politics needs re-examination; for it is a fundamental consideration in statecraft everywhere, all the time.

With economics left out of account, political science cannot rise much above the level of astrology. But when the forms and ownership of property, the productive methods, the economic institutions, and the economic groups and ideas of a given society have been described with the utmost accuracy and when long term trends in the past have been plotted, pure analysis and representative thought have about reached the limits of their procedure. The findings and trends thus disclosed do not constitute an exact science which permits sure predictions as to the definite political consequences that will inexorably flow from the total economic situation or the trends.

Here then we confront the problem of great history, in which all economic, political, military, and other events take place. Inevitably, we also face the central problem of historiography and philosophy: the origin, nature, dynamics, and capacities of human beings in relation to one another and their environment.

But the human mind cannot actually lay hold of things alleged to be "original causes," or things called "causes" in the subsequent flow of personalities and events, and see them functioning independently in particular ways at particular times with inescapable effects discernible to the eye. We cannot picture realistically in the mind economic events or forces operating against "politics" and producing political "effects," as we can, for instance, picture a locomotive coming up behind a train of cars and pushing it ahead to a given destination. Such physical or mechanical images correspond to none of the realities associated with economic interests and activities in conjuncture with political interests and activities.

We may, of course, adopt some such formula as "economics comes first and determines politics." But this is an arbitrary act of will, and the formula is untenable in view of relevant historical knowledge. Human beings had to eat in order to live and they began eating before they established great societies and states; but human beings were more than mere eating-animals even in the most primitive times of which we have knowledge. At an early stage in social evolution, economics and government, such as they were, became inextricably entangled, and their influences upon each other were reciprocal. Not since the beginning of recorded history has this involved relationship been broken: economic changes have affected governments and changes in governments have affected economic institutions and interests. But the problem of which precedes which or what comes first has not been solved by any process of learning or thinking.

Unless we are to remain indefinitely in indecisive meditation upon an unanswerable question, the knot which cannot be unravelled by philosophy or historical inquiry and speculation must be cut by considering the economic basis of politics in terms of action. At bottom, the problem of comprehending, using, and testing the theory or fiction thus becomes one in active statecraft for all reflective persons concerned with living and operating in relation to public affairs. Immediately the theory, which is in itself mere idea, is attached to inner images and impulses and to visible circumstances. Having resolved to act, such persons will clarify their purposes as to economic or political ends, will make use of systematic knowledge and thought relative to economic and political interests, will strive to discern what is inescapable in the given conjuncture of events, and will at length come to a judgment on the general situation with reference to the time and form of proposed actions and their probable consequences.

Stated in another way, the political science of pure thought as an end in itself can ignore the economic basis of politics, but the political science of action cannot—unless forsooth it is wholly irrational and hence doomed to self-destruction. If rational, it will employ systematic knowledge of economic institutions, interests, and forces in all their forms, make conjectures or forecasts derived from this knowledge, reach informed judgments respecting the general situation and its details, make decisions so instructed, take appropriate actions, and submit the outcome to the test of human experience.

But here the absolutist who is sure that he *knows* precisely what will happen in every contingency, real or imagined, will file objections. He will declare that the above conclusion discloses no indefeasible or mathematical laws governing human affairs which will permit certainty in predictions and hence make perfectly plain the right thing to do or say at the right moment in order to accomplish a given end or ends. Besides, he will complain, it introduces the factor of human judgment, which is fallible and belongs to intuition, not knowledge and certainty; it is therefore "mystical" and "unscientific."

To such objections answers are possible. If human affairs are in fact determined under indefeasible or mathematical law, human beings are creatures of fate and have no choices, good or bad, as to the right thing to do or say at any time. They are mere automata in history. With reference to the factor of judgment or intuition, it also appears in the process of formulating theories of physical science, which may or may not be later subjected to the tests of action. At all events, human beings conduct their affairs as if they possess the power of insight, judgment, and choice.

In his volume *The Domain of Natural Science*, one

of the most thoughtful and penetrating works on the subject, E. W. Hobson says (p. 460) that there are two kinds of scientific knowledge: the systematic scheme and the unsystematic synthesis (from which elements of the former may not be absent). "But besides these kinds of knowledge, there exists a kind of apprehension which is more immediate and direct, although it is often inextricably combined with knowledge of the other kinds. This knowledge is given by direct intuition, in which the object in the subject-object relation is apparently apprehended all at once, as a whole, and not by a conscious synthesis of all its parts and their relations. . . . An exceptional power of obtaining an intuitional grasp of a complex as a whole is an essential element in the mental outfit of a man of science of the highest order."

The exercise of "intuitional and imaginative apprehension" is prominent in the history of all the great statecraft that has steered nations through the storms of war and revolution and through years of advancing civilization in times of peace. An example of such statecraft on a large scale is to be found in the proceedings of the men who framed the Constitution of the United States in 1787. These men had at their command knowledge, both systematic and unsystematic; they were familiar with the history of government, tyranny, violence, and liberty; they were intimately acquainted with the political and economic interests involved directly and indirectly in their own undertaking. But, given the nature of their resolve to act, they also had to deal with imponderables, immeasurables, and unpredictables; to make calculations respecting the possibilities and probabilities of the occasion; to pass judgment on the general situation; and finally, without being certain as to the outcome, to make a decision on the forms of actions to be risked, in the hope of attaining the ends of union, government, and liberty, projected in the paper draft of the Constitution submitted to ratifying bodies and to validation by events.

By way of summary, the theory of the economic basis of politics may be restated in the following formulas:

Revolutions and wars on a world-shaking scale have been accompanied by accelerated alterations in the forms and functions of economies and governments.

If historical experience is any guide, drastic changes in economy will find expressions in politics; and, on the other hand, changes in the functions of government will be followed by repercussions in economy.

In every civilized society, whatever the nature, ownership, and law of property, a diversity of economic interests appears and "the most common and durable source" of clashing interests in politics is the various and unequal distribution of property or income (above, pp. 16–19).

The practice of democracy as government by the will of majorities or pluralities, under the theory of free and equal heads, does not eliminate economic interests, prevent collisions among them, or guarantee a pacific conduct of government or an efficient solution of contradictions (above, Chapter IV).

In the absence of military force, economic interests will come to expression in political power.

If private economic interests, having achieved political power, cannot provide an efficient economic underpinning of society in the long run, they will lose their sovereignty to politics or military force.

If by force or stratagem politics achieves sovereignty over all private economic interests, it will have to maintain an efficient economic basis of its own or perish for want of life-giving support.

If military force triumphs over both economics and politics, it must assure an economic basis of its own or collapse amid the ruins of sterile power.

If there are no individual or group economic interests possessing a high degree of independence as against the state, despotism will supplant constitutional government and then run its own historic course.

In the absence of military force, under constitutional government, that is, limited government, against which a high degree of freedom is provided by the supreme law, the statecraft loyal to such government is under obligation to recognize the nature and existence of economic interests, promote certain interests in particular times and circumstances, restrain specific interests in particular times and places, and in general facilitate voluntary and compulsory adjustments of conflicting interests within the framework of some common civil policy.

The principal alternative to such constitutional government and practice of statecraft is the pursuit of specific interests to the bitter end—to the test of sheer power to the uttermost. This will culminate in a resort to arms by one or more of the conflicting interests and may eventuate in the triumph of one among them (or a coalition); or, if long historical experience is conclusive, will result in the destruction of all factions in the ordeal of violence.

The realities to which the above formulas refer come within the sweep of total history in time. They are not self-contained and independent "tracts of matter and force." They are enmeshed in other human characteristics and events—biological, mental, moral, artistic, and religious—that also appear in total history. The origins of total history, like that of the physical universe, are shrouded in the darkness of pre-history, and the law or laws of total history, if there be any, have not been discovered. Given the fragmentary evidences available, these origins and law or laws cannot be discovered by the human mind. Hence the above formulas of economics and politics are not "laws of history" but are in the nature of conditioned and conditional axioms respecting probabilities of high degree, subject to modifications by the acquisition of new knowledge and by the experiences of a future that cannot be forecast with any mathematical or descriptive certainty worthy of the name.